If God
be for us

A Study in the Meaning of Justification

JOSEPH M. SHAW

AUGSBURG PUBLISHING HOUSE
MINNEAPOLIS, MINNESOTA

IF GOD BE FOR US

Copyright © 1966 Augsburg Publishing House

Scripture quotations are from the Revised Standard Version of the Bible, copyright 1946 and 1952 by the Division of Christian Education of the National Council of Churches.

Manufactured in the United States of America

To my daughter
Nancy Joy

Foreword

A tower has both height and strength. Grounded in a firm foundation, it provides the opportunity for a full-range perspective and soaring vision. It was in a tower that Luther had the shattering experience of grace which began the Reformation with its insights into the Gospel of God and new freedoms for man.

Volumes in the Tower Books series aspire to this image. They seek to serve the curious and reflective Christian by examining the varied themes of God and man in clear, concise, and interesting (perhaps even sparkling) ways. Committed to the biblical faith, the various authors explore great ideas, reflect on the application of the faith to daily life, transmit the wisdom of inspiring thinkers in the past, suggest new strategy for the church in the world, and open up the Scriptures as honestly and competently as they can.

Each author is different and writes from his own "tower" and in his own style. You, the reader, read against the background of your own experience, of course.

Being a Christian in the modern age is an exciting enterprise. It requires both diligence and knowledge. For this task we all need the help and counsel of others.

Take and read.

And joy to you!

Kent S. Knutson
Editor, Tower Books

Contents

1.

Everyone Wants to Be Justified

Not everyone has an interest in justification as a special theological term taken from the Bible, but everyone wants to be justified. People who have some familiarity with the language of theology know that justification is a way of speaking about the work of Jesus Christ in making it possible for sinful men to enjoy the right relationship with Almighty God. Others who have either no knowledge or no interest in such religious topics still live in a world where the idea of justification, whether expressed in words or not, is an important part of the mental and emotional texture of daily living. Let us note some examples.

A person doesn't need to know any theology whatever to realize that nations justify their actions to one another. During President Eisenhower's second term there took place the famous U-2 episode which gave the President the task of justifying to the world what that high-soaring plane was doing over Soviet territory. The late Ambassador Adlai Stevenson once displayed large photographs to the United Nations Security Council which showed plainly the Soviet missiles in Cuba, evidence of a military build-up on that island. Hence the United States was justified in imposing an embargo on all shipments to Cuba.

1

Again, there is justification of a nontheological sort in the ordinary business of selling and buying. The merchant justifies the prices he charges by telling us how much he has to pay his help, how his equipment wears out and needs replacing, how taxes are going up, and the like. If the customer does not think that the price is justified, he can always shop around. When you and I ponder our own behavior as customers (or do you prefer "consumers"?) we discover that we are experts in justification. "I was perfectly satisfied with my other car, but I had to trade now in order to get anything out of it." And who is to say that this may not be a perfectly valid justification? People with money to spare and several cars can be exempted, perhaps, but there are still many of us around who feel that a major purchase has to be justified. It is not just a matter of doing this justifying in conversation with friends or neighbors; it is just as important to justify the new car to ourselves.

The things we do call for justification, and so do the words we speak. Public figures are frequently issuing statements to "clarify" some earlier pronouncement. We do the same thing. "I didn't mean to leave the impression that I thought your figures were wrong, Sam. I just think they might need some restudy." Our human instincts tell us that the wrong words might injure a relationship with someone whom we would like to get along with. So we explain what we really meant. We justify our words.

All of these familiar examples are pointing at something which goes deeper. In countless transparent or subtle ways we justify our actions, our decisions, our words, but all the while we are actually justifying our very selves. We claim the right to live, and to live is to be counted, to be recognized as a valid person. Take the casual statement, "I wanted to go to the concert last night but I was too tired." This may be a plain statement of fact, but it may also have behind it a justifying motive which goes something like this: "I want you to know that I too am a cultured person who appreciates fine music. Please do not construe my absence from the concert as an indication that I fall below the rest of you in the aesthetic realm. My not being there was not my fault. An outside factor, exhaustion, kept me from attending. As far as my real self is concerned, I am as culturally alive as ever."

We agree that justifying one's missing a concert does not represent much of a crisis. The threat to the ego is not too serious. When someone directly criticizes or attacks us, though, it is a different story. In the counseling lingo of the day, then we hurt. The harder we are hit, the stronger the impulse to justify ourselves. And it is characteristic that we feel the criticism, not as an attack upon our actions or words alone, but as a threat to our very selves. In moments of pain and anger we wish that there were some kind of public court where we could appear and declare to everyone: "I am not the kind of person my opponent says I am." But there is no such court available to us. We have to find what reassurance we can from family and friends, people who are close to us and who accept us. And even in such surroundings the self-justification goes on. Spouse and friend offer encouragement, but the individual who hurts must still carry on the struggle to accept himself.

That Isn't All Bad

The illustrations I have given thus far seem to be suggesting that when we look at the process of justification in our daily lives we see something suspicious or bad. Perhaps you expect me to write off this non-religious justification as indicating man's sinfulness, thus opening the way to talk about theological justification as the answer to man's unhappy tendency to justify himself. That would provide a fairly tidy scheme for getting into the biblical and theological meaning of justification, but that will come later. Right now we should try to recognize that it isn't all bad when people feel the need to justify themselves. Sometimes it can be bad, as we all know, especially when we ride rough-shod over the facts in order to make ourselves look good. We all know of times when someone's desire to justify himself was so strong that the objective facts in the case were ignored. I would hope to be objective enough to pay the repair bill when my child breaks a neighbor's window and not fall back on that old parental dodge: "My child would never do a thing like that."

When I say that justification in the ordinary, everyday sense of the word is not all bad, I have in mind the fact that human existence is a network of relationships wherein less than perfect people still have to accept responsibility for what they do. It is better that we sense an obligation to do the things which *can* be justified than the opposite. The opposite would be irresponsibility. In the case of a powerful political leader, it could result in tyranny. In the case of the rest of us, the failure to act responsibly could and would bring certain harm, loss, and confusion.

So I suggest, if it does not seem to be claiming too much, that the necessity to justify ourselves and our deeds can actually be seen as a mark of civilization. It implies that others are involved in what we do, therefore we ought to achieve a certain expected standard of performance. Where there is no need whatever to justify, there is chaotic selfishness. But where a community has developed some standards, its members recognize the difference between upholding the agreed-upon level of existence and departures from that level. The one who defies the standards ought to be required to justify his defiance. It happens that the standards themselves need reevaluation from time to time. Creative rebels might succeed in demonstrating the need to alter the standards, but even the rebels are expected to set forth some suggestion of a better way of life for the community.

So the fact that "everyone wants to be justified" is certainly not all bad. Remember, we are saying these things with reference to familiar human experience. I wish to be quite emphatic about this because there is something artificial in deploring all human efforts at self-justification in order to make the case for another kind of justification which comes from the Christian tradition. Instead of drawing a sharp contrast between "ordinary" justification and "theological" justification as two entirely different things, I contend that the basic problem of justification belongs to the human dilemma from which no one is exempted. The theologian has no special license to disregard society's need for justice which, we have noted, comes up for consideration as soon as we see justification in relation to our ordinary responsibilities. It is too easy for the theologian or churchman to make a comfortable distinction between the sacred and the secular also with respect to justification. According to this reasoning, justification in the good sense has to do with religion, with the spiritual sphere, with God. The other kind of justification is mostly bad because it only proves that man is arrogant and sinful, trying to justify himself. As to justice, some would say, that is a wholly secular concept which has nothing to do with man's inner life.

In our day, theology is making a valiant effort to relate itself to the whole range of human life. It is a kind of indulgence to spin off elaborate theological definitions, whether of justification or some other doctrine, and then defend their abstruse character by pleading that theology is sealed off from ordinary discourse and thus claims the right to language and insights open only to the initiates. As to justification, we have a duty to say something about its plain meaning as understood by everyone as well as its more specialized theological meaning as grasped by those who already know the language of the Bible and the church.

We have said that we cannot discuss justification very long before we confront the notion of justice. Now if the church claims to know something special about justification and that special insight cannot be related to the general human desire for justice, then the church must be charged with carrying on a private conversation with itself. Our contention that "everyone wants to be justified" has deliberately avoided theological conceptions so as to show the desire for justification as a common human phenomenon, not just a "doctrine" which can only be treated under church auspices.

Having said that, we must also include church people among those who want to be justified. Therefore it is time to turn to the kind of talk about justification which you will hear in and around the church. May I suggest that as one listens in, he sometimes hears things about justification which miss the point.

Three Ways to Miss the Point

Before being critical, however, we should try to be positive. Now that we are ready to meet some of the more traditional theological language about justification, we should say in a few sentences what justification is. I do not promise to defend the following as my final "definition" of justification. It is too early in the book for that; moreover, definitions as such have a limited usefulness if not accompanied by a discussion of the separate parts of the definition.

"Justification" is a term coming to us from the New Testament where it is used most frequently in the letters of Paul. It is generally understood to mean the gracious act of God by which, through Jesus Christ, he releases man from the guilt of his sin and declares him righteous. The doctrine of justification by faith alone became a keystone of the Protestant Reformation. To this day, Protestants will use the term justification especially when they wish to underscore the fact that man is put in the right before God by faith in Christ and not by his merits or good works. Justification is one of several metaphors or word pictures used by the apostle Paul to describe the Gospel, the good news concerning Jesus Christ and his saving work. If these sentences convey a general idea as to what is meant by justification, they have served their purpose for the time being. Now we have the practical task of pointing out three familiar flaws in the thinking and talking about justification which goes on in church circles.

1. The first way to miss the point is to speak about justification without justice. We touched on this aspect earlier when we described justification in its ordinary, nontheological sense. I have never heard a pastor or other Christian teacher present justification in

a way that deliberately omits the consideration of justice. The omission is there nevertheless, however unintended, however unconsciously transmitted. The net effect of some discussions of justification is to convey the notion that because Christ makes possible the justification of the sinner (good biblical teaching), we are free to forget God's demands for justice (unbiblical teaching). As a matter of fact, the impression is left that God has lost interest in justice—he no longer requires it.

Apparently the Bible is the story of how God has changed. Once, long ago, he said, "Let justice roll down like waters, and righteousness like an ever-flowing stream" (Amos 5:24), but now he feels less strongly about justice. Or so we are led to assume.

Along with the omission of God's demand for justice comes a virtual omission of God himself. Justification becomes exclusively associated with God's Son, Jesus Christ, and the only part God the Father plays is that of a remote deity who is made to compare unfavorably with the Son. Christ is all generosity and forgiveness; God, on the other hand, lurks threateningly in the background as the stern opposite to the kindly Christ. God and his demand for justice really belong to the past.

Heaven, not earth, is what immediately comes to mind for many when we speak about justification. That this is the case is no accident; much of our childhood religious training went out of its way to name heaven as the sphere where all realities connected with God are to be found. As Joseph Stump puts it in his Explanation of Luther's Small Catechism, " . . . those who believe in Christ are *justified* for His sake; that is, they are pronounced by God to be righteous and fit to enter into heaven."[1] I should not want to argue that justification has nothing to do with the life to come because it most emphatically does (see Gal. 5:5). Nor can one deny that the phrase "pronounced by God to be righteous" could, with proper interpretation, be related to the implementing of justice here on earth. What I fear is that the statement as a whole seems to be saying that the point of being justified is to be made fit to enter into heaven. Our concern should be to include both heaven and earth in the meaning of justification. I am of the opinion that much of the talk about justification is so exclusively heaven-directed that we lose sight of earthly responsibilities. Here on earth there is a crying, weeping, suffering need for justice. Who is better equipped to work for justice than those who have been justified in Christ? Furthermore, those who have met Christ know more about justice than the world does. They can teach the world that justice ultimately means, not simply keeping some semblance of order in a mixed-up world, but carrying out the positive will of God here on earth. "Thy kingdom come, thy will be done on earth as it is in heaven." There will be more to say about this later.

2. The second way to miss the point about justification is to explain it apart from the grace of God in Christ Jesus. Justification without grace describes another unintended state of affairs reflected in church talk about justification. To put the matter provocatively, justification by faith is in one sense a half-truth. I shall defend this statement in due course, but first allow me to set the stage for what I want to say by taking a paragraph for a little demonstration which will show how plausible the "half-truth" can appear.

You are the class and I'll be the teacher and we will now turn to our lesson for today, "Justification by Faith." Way back in history the children of Israel re-

ceived certain revelations from God. Among them was
the law, given through Moses as God's explicit commands to be obeyed. The Israelites tried to keep the
Law, but they failed. God sent them prophets to warn
of the consequences of disobedience, but still they
failed, again and again. Finally, after many centuries,
God saw that this approach wouldn't work at all, so he
sent his Son Jesus and his servant Paul with a fresh
revelation and a new teaching. Jesus and Paul taught
that what mattered to God was not whether we obeyed
the Law or not, but whether we had faith. Many of the
people were overjoyed to hear this good news, and
they came to be known as Christians. They had faith,
which was what God wanted. They tried to tell the
others that obedience to the Law was no longer the
key to getting along with God. That key was faith. The
Jews for the most part didn't believe this, and went
on trying to perform good works. The centuries sped
by, and Christian teaching became weak and diluted
with the result that many were now back at the old
grind of trying to earn salvation by works. Things were
in sorry shape until Martin Luther came along. He read
Paul and other parts of the Bible and announced,
"Look, folks, we've been doing this all wrong. The
Bible says that God wants faith, not a lot of works.
Just have faith and the works will follow of themselves."
That was the Reformation. Ever since, those Christians
who know their Bibles and follow the Reformers have
taught that justification is by faith. End of lesson.

I hope you will not be offended at the way I am
trying to make this point. The paragraph above, as you
have sensed, is a device. It is a caricature of Protestant
thinking and teaching about justification. Other biblical teachings are also handled in a dubious way, but
let us stick to justification. If you will bear with me,

let us ask the question, What is wrong with the above presentation of justification? Surely it makes the point that justification is by faith and not by works. You know you are being taken in, but in what respect? Taking one of the less harmful distortions first, the so-called explanation of justification in our "lesson" pictured faith as something which a person is supposed to "have" much as one "has" a haircut or "has" a new watch, whereas we know that faith is a profound trust in God.

But much more serious is the other distortion. What is missing in our contrived "lesson" on justification? *Nothing less than the entire substance of Christianity is missing!* Jesus is mentioned in passing as God's Son, true enough, but his role is simply that of a teacher. There is not one reference to that which is at the heart of the ministry of Jesus Christ, namely, his cross and resurrection. To put it another way, there is no mention of the *grace* of God. In the New Testament and Christian sense, the grace of God is set forth in the person and work of Jesus Christ. To say that Jesus, with Paul, taught that man should have faith is to bypass the central meaning of Christ's entire ministry, which includes his passion and resurrection.

A third distortion goes back to the treatment of faith. The announcement that now man is to have faith is regarded as the transmission of another piece of information. We are not told what or whom we are to have faith in, nor why. Faith is apparently a self-explanatory quality which men can acquire at any time and at will. The Gospel, on the other hand, makes clear that God works faith in man's mind and heart by placing before man a persuasive message about God's great deed of love.

For all the exaggeration of my little "lesson," I fear

If God Be for Us

that many of our friends who feel that they are well
posted on such matters are actually the victims of serious misunderstanding. They are pleased to have discovered that the formula "justification by faith" has
biblical support plus the endorsement of a great teacher
like Luther. "Faith" is taken as a good word to know
as over against the discredited notion of "works."
Faith may mean something roughly equivalent to "sincerity," or it may mean an attitude which stands in
general agreement with the teachings of the Bible and
the church. In the latter case, "to have faith" is regarded as having undergone the normal indoctrination
in Christian teaching and having concluded this training
without rejecting it. It is a satisfaction to them that
they have been let in on the secret of what God really
wants. God wants faith, so the sensible person gets
faith. Then God is pleased.

There are others, though, who would not fall prey
to such superficial reasoning. They know something
about the quality of faith. Faith is not simply acquies-
cence in the teaching of the church. It is much more
personal than that. Faith is, in fact, a personal trust in
God. This is a significant step forward in defining
faith, for faith is indeed personal trust, personal commitment, a complete willingness to rest in God. But
the same error is still possible, namely, the error of
regarding the faith which justifies as stemming from
the self and being credited, ultimately, to one's own
decision to have it. So even a greatly improved, personal defining of faith may still leave the individual
in the same dilemma of taking satisfaction in this trusting quality he has acquired rather than finding his faith
rooted in grace; that is, in the specific action of God
in Christ which is the root and source of faith.

The answer to the dilemma can be found in these

words from Ephesians: "For by grace you have been saved through faith; and this is not your own doing, it is the gift of God" (Eph. 2:8). Before commenting on these words let us bring in a sentence from Romans: "they are justified by his grace as a gift, through the redemption which is in Christ Jesus" (Rom. 3:24). Salvation and justification, then, are *by grace*. Yes, justification by grace comes "through faith," but the controlling idea is *grace*. Grace can be thought of as biblical shorthand for God's saving act in Jesus Christ. Grace is what makes the difference between being a Christian and not being one. "But by the grace of God I am what I am, and his grace toward me was not in vain" (1 Cor. 15:10). Grace is what does the saving work; faith appropriates what Christ has done. Faith is man's response to the offered gift, "justified by his grace as a gift."

Therefore faith must not be construed as a desirable human quality which God rewards with justification, or salvation, or some other benefit. The great lesson of Paul, recovered by Luther, can so easily be spoiled when man mentally calculates that faith is a new commodity which God has agreed to accept in return for man's redemption. There was faith in the Old Testament, but not the grace of God revealed in Christ. Indeed, there was grace too in the Old Testament, but not the grace of God focused and embodied and given in Jesus Christ.

A final observation to be made here is that when we exalt justification by faith we must make sure that we do not regard this tremendous insight as a simple substitution of one word for another, "faith" for "works." These are not merely two different words; they represent totally different interpretations of religion. If the secret of salvation were to be seen as knowing the right word, then we should be back to another version of good works as the basis for God's favor. I hope the main point is clear: the grounds for our justification is the grace of God in Jesus Christ. Faith is only the reception of the gift, and Ephesians tells us that God himself brings about the receptivity: "this is not your own doing."

3. There is a third way of missing the point of justification. The first had to do with God, the second with Christ, and sure enough, the third has to do with the Holy Spirit. We are warning against "justification without justice," against "justification without grace"; now we must caution against "justification without fellowship." This warning may not be as readily discernible, but it is relatively simple to remind ourselves that the Holy Spirit is linked in Scripture with the fellowship of believers. Take the familiar apostolic benediction, for example: "The grace of the Lord Jesus Christ and the love of God and the fellowship of the Holy Spirit be with you all" (2 Cor. 13:14).

What kind of distortion are we trying to describe when we say that we must not conceive of justification without fellowship? My reply is that we so often hear justification described as a private transaction between God and the sinner, and that this is really a misunderstanding. First we are swift to agree that genuine religious experience will always have something of "aloneness" about it. Luther remarks, for example, that the experience of death brings out the solemn aloneness of the believer before God. But it is also Luther who teaches us so much, and so eloquently, about the fellowship of believers. In this life we are not alone, nor should we seek to be. Granted, the decision to believe in Christ is a decision I must make and you must make. The parents cannot decide for the child, the church cannot decide for its members. If my faith is the genuine article, it is profoundly *my* faith, and not a transaction which someone else or the Christian congregation enters into on my behalf. We are right in linking this insistence on personal accountability before God with the New Testament writings and with classical Reformation teaching.

It often happens, however, that a most valuable insight is driven out of its original relationship with the rest of Christian teaching. The first Christians, as they thought about justification, recognized as a matter of course that this was an experience which they all shared in common. Modern Christians, with quite a different background, tend to see justification as something which people experience in separation from one another. The apostle Paul uses the plural quite easily: "they are justified" (Rom. 3:24), "we are justified" (Rom. 5:1). Christians in our day, on the other hand, find it natural to use the pronoun "I" in connection with justification.

The whole matter of communal and individual religious experience could be the subject of a lengthy essay in itself. For the most part, Protestants have a distinct bias in favor of the individual expression of faith, and this bias shows up when justification is being considered. But if we are open to the evidence of the New Testament, we can appreciate that justification, too, belongs to "the fellowship of the Holy Spirit." Faith is indeed a *personal* matter, but it is not thereby a *private* matter. It is a good thing to hold to personal religion as over against a detached, impersonal religion which is supposed to have validity even though it remains somewhere outside of my inmost being. But it is an unhealthy thing to interpret faith and justification as totally private concerns between me and

God, disregarding the presence and reality of the Christian community.

Now we may examine briefly the Pauline perspective on justification as a work of God which nourishes unity in the church. When Paul was first contending for justification by grace through faith, he was thinking about the membership of the church. Specifically, he was attacking discrimination against Gentiles on the part of those Jewish Christians who wanted the Gentile Christians to adopt certain old Jewish practices, particularly circumcision. The second chapter of Galatians clearly shows us that the issue which prompted Paul to come out strongly for justification by faith in Christ was the issue of fellowship in the church.

First, says Paul, he and his fellow missionary Barnabas had been given "the right hand of fellowship" (Gal. 2:9) which meant that it was agreed that those two should take the Gospel to the Gentile world. But, he continues, Cephas (another name for Peter) acted inconsistently with the agreement, for when an occasion arose for him to demonstrate his conviction that the Gospel was for all men, he was ashamed to have his Jerusalem colleagues see him in actual fellowship with Gentiles.

From all this we can only conclude, as several scholars nowadays have been showing us, that as far as Paul was concerned, justification is to be brought into the picture to secure and maintain genuine fellowship in the church. Jesus Christ has wiped out the line of distinction between Jew and Gentile. Now the two groups stand on common ground: justification by faith. Before, the differences between Jews and Gentiles were the center of attention. Now, the differences have been rendered irrelevant, giving way to an incomparably greater fact, their oneness in Christ.

In pointing to the inadequacy of "justification without fellowship" we have introduced important historical evidence that this doctrine appears within the setting of the first-century problem of uniting Jewish and Gentile believers. But what does this observation have to say to us? Even though our circumstances are quite different, the church of the twentieth century has staked out Christian unity as one of its most important challenges. Therefore the principle of justification still has a significant job to do in modern Christianity, and there are encouraging signs that Roman Catholics and Protestants are anxious to lay aside old polemics in an effort to understand one another's views on justification.

But striking closer to the arena of daily living, consider the practical relevance of justification *with* fellowship. Two things happen when justification is lived out in the church. First, the church demonstrates the reality of the Gospel by hailing the disappearance of old barriers to fellowship. Since justification is by faith, and not by works, by education, by wealth, by race, by age, or by sex, the world takes note of the power of Christ to bring men together. Second, the individual himself discovers the concrete, human reality of acceptance. It is small comfort to the lonely, isolated, friendless person to be told, "It's too bad that everyone rejects you, but at least God accepts you." That would be a partial Gospel. Justification in the New Testament sense never means that God puts one in the right but then leaves him to wander the earth alone. No! Justification includes the experience of fellowship in the company of the church, here and now! It is important for you and for me to discover that we are accepted in a fellowship of human beings who care for us.

If you have tasted the joys of genuine Christian fellowship, I don't have to convince you that there is more to it than mere chumminess or togetherness. The church is an organism tough enough to sustain its members in their deepest sorrows as well as in their moments of greatest joy. Its toughness is also seen in relation to justification. Undoubtedly many other societies cultivate "acceptance" in the sense that the members are urged to be kindly disposed to one another. The church goes far beyond acceptance as an attitude closely akin to toleration. "In Christ Jesus you are all sons of God, through faith," writes Paul (Gal. 3:26). What this means is that through justification we receive a new standing as persons. We may put this a bit stronger: in Christ we become authentic persons. So, in a sense, there *is* a public court where we can present our case and be justified; the church serves as such a place. In the fellowship of Christ's followers we experience at first hand that our lives have validity, that we count as full human beings. Here is an aspect of justification which our generation should more fully explore.

Everyone wants to be justified. Or so we have said. Has the point been proved? We have had no surveys or statistics to work from. We have simply claimed that people both outside and within the church have a desire, however unconscious it may be, to feel that they are in the right. It matters little whether the words "justify" and "justification" are used when we are examining a common human trait. As a matter of fact, I suspect that those very words *are* used a great deal, quite apart from any effort to speak theologically. My plan in this chapter has been to say something first about this non-theological awareness of justification which runs through our ordinary, day-to-day existence. I have suggested that we should take a look at this phenomenon before we hoist our theological armor into place to do battle against it. That people seek to justify themselves can indeed be taken as a signal to gallop forth waving the banner of biblical justification. It also happens to be a sign of man's effort to establish a measure of order in his world. This effort is directly bound up with man's age-old search for justice, a search in which Christians share and to which they should contribute the special knowledge concerning justice which proceeds from the Bible.

The second part of this chapter had us listening in on three inadequate ideas about justification which float around when this topic is taken up in church circles. These three notions were prefaced by a provisional summary of the doctrine of justification. We wanted to be positive, you'll recall, before being critical. But it was necessary to point out the weaknesses of "the three ways to miss the point." Justification, after all, has a direct kinship with justice. Moreover, its New Testament meaning requires that we relate it to the grace of God in Jesus Christ, lest we merely engage in word play, substituting "faith" as an improved version of "works." Finally, we went back to a couple of key spots in Paul's letters to discover that he understood and taught justification in the context of fellowship in the church.

People want to be justified, whoever they are. Those outside the church are not aware that their natural desire for justification is at heart a theological matter. And some who are within the church have missed the point as to what justification means. What we need to do next is to turn to Scripture's declaration about justification.

2.

Everyone Can Be Justified

By this time the title of this chapter may seem like a foregone conclusion. The claim that everyone can be justified strikes one as familiar Christian teaching. The reader of the New Testament knows that in Paul's letter to the Romans, for example, the "all" who are under the power of sin or the "all" who have sinned and fallen short of the glory of God (Rom. 3:9, 23) can become the ones who "are justified by [God's] grace as a gift, through the redemption which is in Christ Jesus" (Rom. 3:24). But since we are on familiar ground, let us make sure we follow the New Testament also in underscoring that justification for all is to be treated as a *possibility*—something all can and may experience, but not something which automatically takes place. After all, "we are justified by faith." Everyone *can* be justified; it depends on man's willingness to receive the gift of justification if in fact everyone *will* be justified.

The title of this chapter, then, announces two things. It paraphrases the good news that what Christ has done for men is available for everyone. It also declares, through the inclusion of the little word "can," that men are asked to open themselves to the gift of justification.

The Good News as Surprise

There is always a surprise element in good news, despite our familiarity with the factual elements of it. The child knows perfectly well that his birthday is day after tomorrow and that the birthday party will mean a cake, candles, presents, and balloons. Still there is delighted surprise registered in the shining eyes when the happy occasion arrives. The favored political candidate knows from the polls that a comfortable margin of victory seems assured. On election day he follows the returns hour by hour and discovers that he is in fact outdistancing his closest opponent. But for all that, it is good news for him and his supporters when election is assured, and the celebration swings into high gear when the announcement is made that he has won.

In innumerable cases where people are given good news, the surprised reaction is again and again expressed in such exclamations as "It seems too good to be true" and "I just can't believe it." If we ask, "When are these exclamations heard?" the answer is: when the good news actually happens. The day of the birthday party finally arrives; the election returns are completed and announced; a salesman actually obtains that large order; the actress hears her name being announced as the winner of an Academy Award.

These illustrations might help us to appreciate that when the good news of Jesus Christ reaches its mark, it is an event. If we are church people or Bible readers, we become familiar with the spoken or written forms of the announcement that God loved sinners to the extent that he sent his Son to save them. But our familiarity turns to delighted surprise when this announcement becomes a happening in our lives. As we now proceed into this second chapter, where we will look at the biblical teaching of justification, I offer the suggestion that justification has a special suitability for translating a Gospel grown perhaps too familiar into a surprising event in our lives. The Gospel of God's love in Jesus Christ has the quality of surprise only when the message gets through, and justification will help it get through. If we can avoid making justification itself into something all too familiar, it can become the cutting edge of the Gospel's axe, the sharp point of the Gospel's needle.

Surprise in the Old Testament

Even the Old Testament can shed important light on the meaning of justification. We say "even" because a favorite fallacy is the notion that the Old Testament is a gloomy collection of laws and threats from which the reader flees in dread in order to find solace in the more friendly New Testament. No, the Old Testament too records the actions of a gracious God. More than that, we need the Old Testament to help us see the point of justification as taught by Paul in the New Testament.

A reading of the Old Testament makes the story of Jesus Christ believable because it acquaints us with a God who takes action in human history. God summoned Abraham and Jacob to be the ancestors of his chosen people. The crowning demonstration of God's willingness to save is his deliverance of the children of Israel from Egypt. In the Old Testament scheme of things, God's greatest redemptive act comes early in the story; the rest of the narrative describes Israel's struggle to come to terms with the meaning of God's initial deeds of freeing and establishing the people whom he had chosen to be his servant. These deeds are known as the Exodus and the giving of the Covenant.

Many people seem to lose sight of the Covenant because they become diverted by the Ten Commandments. In fact, many are unable to comprehend that the God of the Old Testament is a God of grace because they only remember the giving of the Ten Commandments followed by Israel's prompt lapse into idolatry. The concentration on the Ten Commandments in Sunday school instruction and in popular filmed presentations leaves on thousands of minds the impression that God is primarily a demanding God who made his nature clear by issuing ten inflexible commands which raise a mighty standard of perfection against which we are measured to our shame. But God is primarily a God who graciously gives a covenant to his people. How easily we miss the significance of the words which introduce the Ten Commandments: "I am the Lord your God, who brought you out of the land of Egypt, out of the house of bondage" (Ex. 20:2). And the Commandments themselves were not intended as a burden; they were intended for Israel's good. God desired that his people should experience a good life under his care and leadership.

But what can all this indicate about justification? And where is the surprise? We must not expect to find the identical teaching on justification which the New Testament offers appearing before us in the Old Testament. However, we shall find an important connection by singling out one particular term which is related to justification. The term to examine at this point is "righteousness." A look at this term in the Old Testament should yield a surprise of considerable importance.

Our religious musings are so cramped under the weight of conventional ideas that we are seldom pre-

pared for the surprises Scripture has for us. We like
to think that we already know what the Bible will say,
so we do not bother to listen to what it is saying. What
comes to mind when we consider "righteousness"?
Well, the idea that God is righteous, that righteousness
is associated with his holy character, and that he looks
for righteousness in the lives of his children. Correct
on all counts. So where is the surprise? To answer that
we need to place some specific verses before us.

First, we might observe that righteousness can appear in the company of some other important words,
as in Psalm 89:14:

> Righteousness and justice are the
> foundation of thy throne;
> steadfast love and faithfulness go
> before thee.

From this verse we learn that "righteousness" need
not keep exclusive company with such concepts as
wrath, punishment, and the like, though we rather expect it to. Here righteousness is mentioned along with
justice, to be sure, but also with love and faithfulness.

A verse from another Psalm points to further interesting associations. "He has distributed freely, he has
given to the poor; his righteousness endures for ever"
(Psalm 112:9). Here the righteous man is the subject,
"the man who deals generously and lends" (v. 5). Perhaps we are prepared to read something like this, for
righteousness on the part of a man would have to
imply a certain mode of upright behavior. Yet it is interesting that the mark of a righteous person is seen in
his generosity, his care of the poor. The same thought
comes to light in the case of a righteous king, according to Psalm 72. We quote the first two verses:

Give the king thy justice, O God,
and thy righteousness to the royal son!
May he judge thy people with righteousness,
and thy poor with justice!

And the Psalmist goes on a little later:

May he defend the cause of the poor
   of the people,
give deliverance to the needy,
and crush the oppressor!

God gives his righteousness to the king so that he
may judge God's people with righteousness. In carrying out this kind of judgment, the king goes to the aid
of the needy, delivering them from their oppressors.
As we know, the great prophets of Israel, such as
Isaiah, constantly took their people to task for their
lack of righteousness, and this is exactly what they had
in mind: the failure to espouse the cause of the poor
and needy. Consider these lines in Isa. 3:13-15:

The Lord has taken his place to contend,
   he stands to judge his people.
The Lord enters into judgment
   with the elders and princes of his
   people:
"It is you who have devoured the
vineyard,
   the spoil of the poor is in your
   houses.
What do you mean by crushing my
people,
   by grinding the face of the poor?"
   says the Lord God of hosts.

Righteousness on the part of men, we may readily
conclude, does not mean an abstract sense of justice,

nor is it a narrowly "religious" idea having to do with a man's formal relationship with God. Rather it is a very concrete matter, packed with down-to-earth ethical demands. To show righteousness is to help those who are in need, to look after the poor.

The next step is to illustrate how God himself shows righteousness in the same way. The Old Testament believers knew this to be the case. They did not think, as we are sometimes led to believe, that the righteousness of God is the sum total of all that is terrible and frightening about the Almighty. Those who trusted in him actually appealed to his righteousness. "In thee, O Lord, do I take refuge; let me never be put to shame! In thy righteousness deliver me and rescue me; incline thy ear to me, and save me!" (Psalm 71: 1-2).

Let us put our imaginations to work for a moment. It is as if a friend has urged us to visit a nearby park where there is a particularly impressive statue. It is entitled "Righteousness," he says, and we must by all means go over and see it. So we walk over to the park in the late afternoon, and sure enough, there stands the great statue, looming magnificently against the sky. At first we cannot make out the details, since it is silhouetted against the setting sun. However, we gather from the general profile that a fearsome warrior, a veritable giant of a figure, is standing with uplifted sword, poised to destroy in a single stroke the enemy cowering at his feet. But as we walk around the statue, getting the light of the sun at our backs so as to let it illumine the details, we catch our breaths at the sight. The towering figure is not a warrior, and he is not striking his enemy. Instead he is a shepherd. What looked like an uplifted sword from one side turns out to be a shepherd's staff. Now we see that "Righteousness" is a shepherd in the act of rescuing his lambs from a dangerous crevice. "In thy righteousness deliver me and rescue me."

We shall make a return visit to the Old Testament when we report how Martin Luther learned a similar thing about righteousness from his reading of the Psalms. It only remains to suggest that our excursion has shown us that God's righteousness, without losing any of its awesome ethical rigor, turns out to be that quality or disposal on God's part which is directly related to the act of delivering the one who calls upon him. It would not be wrong to say that God's righteousness is the theme of the entire Old Testament. Israel's story is the story of God delivering or vindicating his people, thus showing himself to be a righteous God.

That, I believe, is the surprise. When we read the Old Testament with our eyes open, we come away with a distinctly different idea about the righteousness of God. We were well versed in the first lesson concerning God's righteousness. That is, we expected him to reflect his holiness in the requirements he laid upon his people. Further, we expected him to urge righteousness as the proper quality of human relationships. What we didn't expect, though, was that righteousness has another side. To put the matter succinctly, righteousness is not only demand, it is also gift. Because God is righteous, he shows compassion and effects deliverance. Because believing man receives righteousness from God, he takes an active interest in the poor and the oppressed. The ethical side of righteousness is still present. What may surprise us is that righteousness, instead of being an abstract standard against which God judges our success or failure in keeping his law, is seen to be the disposition of God—the very action of God—to extend help to us.

Two Pictures of the Judge

Basic to the process of reading the Bible with profit is the willingness to recognize and correct the caricatures we habitually form concerning certain biblical teachings. We have cited a number of passages from the Old Testament in order to unveil the other side— the gracious side—of God's righteousness. It is tempting to raise the issue whether we have subconsciously conditioned ourselves to come at the Bible with purely moralistic assumptions: the Bible tells us what to do and it is up to us to do it. Or, especially when we are thinking about justification, we readily picture God as the Judge and ourselves as prisoners at the bar of justice.

We ought to look into this notion of God as Judge for a moment. Without any prompting, our minds construct the scene. God sits on the judge's bench, holding court, and the prisoners stand quaking in his majestic presence with dread and foreboding, fearing his awesome authority to pronounce sentence against them. This is not a picture without some biblical support. The following sentences from the prophecy of Malachi give fitting expression to the conception of God as a formidable judge facing the guilty offenders brought before his judgment seat.

> Then I will draw near to you for judgment; I will be a swift witness against the sorcerers, against the adulterers, against those who swear falsely, against those who oppress the hireling in his wages, the widow and the orphan, against those who thrust aside the sojourner, and do not fear me, says the Lord of hosts (Mal. 3:5).

The verse should be read very carefully because there is something there which we will want to come back to in a moment. But now we want to look at another picture of God as judge.

Someone might be thinking about those hearty, sword-wielding military leaders whose mighty exploits are told in the Old Testament Book of Judges. What colorful figures they were! Their ranks even included a remarkable woman, Deborah, along with the noble Gideon who had a chance to be king but refused it. Then there is the less significant but endlessly fascinating Samson, the man of gigantic strength, gigantic appetites, and medium-sized discernment. We hear little if anything about these people holding court. Their task was to deliver the Israelites from their enemies. In a sense they were saviors of their people. "Then the Lord raised up judges, who saved them out of the power of those who plundered them" (Judges 2:16). This is important to notice—that a judge was one who effected deliverance—but it is still not the picture we are looking for.

In ancient times the judge did not hear cases and mete out impartial justice in the manner we would associate with a judge. For one thing, instead of in a courtroom it was more likely that the judge sat at the gate of the village, as Job did before he was afflicted (see Job 29:7-25). And what did the judge do? What was his role in the community? Again we may consult this same chapter in the Book of Job. "I delivered the poor who cried, and the fatherless who had none to help him," says Job.

The ancient judge was anything but impartial as he carried out his role among the people. He was partial! He *favored* the poor, the fatherless, the lame, and the blind. His role was to help. The judge was not supposed to check his human instincts in the interests of neutrality. Instead, he was expected to befriend those who had no friends, to see that the downtrodden were not further victimized, to espouse the cause of any who were in trouble and need. To act in such a way was to "judge," to exercise "righteousness," to secure "justice." It is quite a different image from that of the formidable figure who lays aside his natural compassion in order better to judge impartially.

Our first picture, that of God as a judge of severity, found some validation in the Malachi passage cited above. But I suggested a careful reading of that passage because on closer examination it does not merely typify the judge's function as that of dispensing stern justice. When we first read the passage our impulse is to think to ourselves, "Typical stuff. God the judge is against the sinners." On closer examination, however, the Malachi passage shows God as one who is not only *against* the sinners, but *for* those who are being misused. Indeed God draws near to judge the sorcerers, adulterers, and those who swear falsely, but the list goes on. The judge promises to act "against those who oppress the hireling in his wages, the widow and the orphan." So here again is the theme of the judge as one who looks after the interests of the disinherited.

Our "two pictures of the judge" are not complete opposites. Severity and compassion are both present in God's work as judge. The two pictures do fulfill the practical purpose of bringing out the two aspects of God's justice, however. The portrait of the judge as stern punisher of offenders stresses that side of justice which is concerned with restraining the sinner; the portrait of the judge as champion of the helpless and needy stresses the side of justice which is concerned with righting the wrongs suffered by those who are sinned against. We are not proposing that the idea of righteous judgment should be so revised that we discard the "stern" aspect and retain only the "kindly" aspect. Nor is anything gained by an innocuous balancing of the one aspect against the other. We are characteristically too adept at blunting biblical truth by that device. What emerges from our consideration of God as judge is the insight into the breadth of God's righteousness, and with that insight comes an implication for our study of justification.

Two Sides of Sin

Our theme in this chapter is that everyone can be justified. Even the Old Testament points in that direction if we learn how to look for the evidences of God's grace and kindness in the history of Israel. And as we have seen, God's righteousness is not constricted to a justice to be feared; it is also expressive of God's disposition to come to the aid of the needy in order to deliver them. "In thy righteousness deliver me" (Psalm 71:2) captures in a phrase what we have discovered as to the gracious aspect of divine righteousness.

Our search for biblical light on the theme of justification requires a short study of the biblical way of understanding sin. Not a few theologians in our day interpret justification as equivalent to the forgiveness of sins. Whether they are right or not, and I don't think they are, it is necessary to recognize the human problem of sin if one is to appreciate the good news that God is willing to justify sinners. The fact of sin plays into our discussion of justification even if forgiveness does not, in my judgment, exhaust the meaning of being justified.

Without the light of Scripture on the problem, most people who do any thinking whatever about sin are inclined to define it as the doing of wrong things. To sin is to misbehave, goes the general, popular reasoning. When the sin problem is seen as the problem of misbehavior, then the solution would seem to be a greater exercise of self-control. Don't do it. Other people, with a little more training in the Bible, realize that it isn't that simple. "All men are sinners," they say. Even though a person thinks he is leading an upright life, he is bound to slip at least once in a while. (A profound biblical truth about man blandly transmuted into a specious maxim, as if the universality of sin merely means that everyone makes an occasional mistake!) At best, this view represents an effort to be biblical, but the error is still that of viewing sin as basically the committing of misdeeds.

The idea that all men are sinners obviously stems from the Pauline thought expressed in Rom. 3:23, "All have sinned and fall short of the glory of God." The first part of Paul's statement agrees with the comment above that everyone does in fact sin. But the second part adds another dimension. In falling short of the glory of God, man proves to be less than God meant him to be. His sinful actions are not dismissed lightly. They point to man's refusal to recognize God as God. Sinful acts represent man's rebellion against God, the proud attempt to set himself up as the one who determines what is right. More than that, though, sinful and sinning man misses his true destiny which is to be the glory of God here on earth. God intended that his glory be displayed in human history in and through the life of man.

"Glory of God" is a term both venerable and vague; it is saying something important, but what? Of course, the term suggests God's radiance and splendor; we would all agree that God is glorious in his majesty, power, and holiness. But the history of the term also makes room for God's glory being manifested on earth among men, as the stories of the tabernacle and temple make clear. Since the word "glory" in the Hebrew language has the meaning of weight, mass, substance, or heaviness, we are able to gather from biblical history that when God reveals his glory he is making his presence felt, he is throwing his weight around! In God's long-range scheme, that weight is the earthly life of man; man is to be God's glory, the impact of the reality of God.

We return to Paul's point that the seriousness of sin is the damage it inflicts upon man's noble destiny. "All have sinned and fall short of the glory of God." Thus "falling short of the glory of God" is not to be minimized and reduced to just another way of talking about misconduct. While it is true that sin involves wrong actions, the more serious issue is that man has perversely spoiled his place in God's plan and in the process has even tried to usurp God's place.

Sometimes it is said that man's problem is not only that he sins, but that he is in or has a sinful condition. Or the distinction is offered that sinful actions flow from a basically sinful attitude. Sometimes the singular "sin" is used to apply to this wrong orientation or attitude, while the plural "sins" is reserved to apply to the individual acts of transgression. These modes of expression assist us in learning the Bible's language about the problem of sin. There are two sides to the matter: man commits sinful acts, and man is guilty of a wrong attitude toward God. Justification addresses itself to both sides of sin. In justifying the ungodly, God offers forgiveness in Jesus Christ. Forgiveness covers both one's sinful actions and one's wrong orientation toward God, that is, one's sinful condition. But justification is not limited to forgiveness; justification also addresses itself to the recovery of man's forfeited destiny. Justified through the grace of God in Christ, man is set free to realize his true being which, in God's purpose, is to bring the weight of God to bear upon human history.

We must insist that the realization of this high purpose of man takes place only through the person and work of Jesus Christ. Against the background of our earlier discussion of the righteousness of God, it is instructive to note that the writer of the First Epistle of John refers to Jesus Christ as "the righteous." "If any one does sin, we have an advocate with the Father, Jesus Christ the righteous; and he is the expiation for our sins, and not for ours only but also for the sins of the whole world" (1 John 2:1b-2). The centrality of Christ for justification will be made explicit as we now pursue a study of some important Pauline passages.

The Meaning of a Word

Surprisingly, the Revised Standard Version of the New Testament gives us only three passages where the word "justification" occurs. First we may take Gal. 2:21 which reads, "I do not nullify the grace of God; for if *justification* were through the law, then Christ died to no purpose." This statement affirms, first, that what Paul had said earlier in the same chapter about justification and faith cannot be construed as going against the grace of God, and second, that justification is not through the law.

The other two occurrences of "justification" are in Romans. Rom. 4:25 states that Jesus our Lord "was put to death for our trespasses and raised for our *justification.*" This phrase divides so nicely into two parts that one is inclined at first glance to associate Christ's death with the sin problem, leaving the resurrection to be linked specifically with justification. However, that would be ascribing to Paul a tidy distinction he did not intend. Death and resurrection belong together; it is because Paul has earlier used the story of Abraham's faith in the promise of a son that it is fitting to mention Christ's resurrection along with our justification. Rom. 4:25 offers an example of "synthetic parallelism," where one central thought is stated in two parallel expressions.[1] That main thought is that in our case, too, faith (in the crucified and risen Christ) will be reckoned as righteousness.

The third place where the Revised Standard Version speaks of justification is Rom. 5:16 where the apostle's words are: "For the judgment following one trespass brought condemnation, but the free gift following many trespasses brings *justification*." Throughout Rom. 5 Paul draws contrasts between the one man Adam and the one man Jesus Christ. In verse 15 the free gift of God's grace expressed in the man Jesus Christ is contrasted with the trespass of Adam. There is another contrast in verse 16, cited above: justification is the opposite of the condemnation which followed upon the trespass of Adam. This verse supports our earlier contention that justification is dependent on the grace of God; it is not a reward bestowed upon man because his faith is accepted as a meritorious quality.

It so happens that there are three different Greek words, each of which can be translated "justification," in the three passages we have just examined. Without imposing on the reader's patience too much, we can set forth the situation by the device of listing the passages and the transliterated Greek words, with the briefest explanation, as follows:

Gal. 2:21	*Dikaiosune.*	This word, as the footnote in RSV mentions, is most commonly translated "righteousness." Paul uses this important word something like 34 times.
Rom. 4:25	*Dikaiosis.*	A very authoritative theological lexicon tells us that this word "means the act of justification by the divine acquittal *and with reference to the whole existence of man before God.*"[2] (Italics mine.)
Rom. 5:16	*Dikaioma.*	The same lexicon defines this word as "statute," "requirement," or "ordinance." When Paul uses it of Christ, he means a "right act" in fulfillment of legal requirement.[3] Notice again that in this verse it stands as the opposite of condemnation.

Those are the three verses we began with, all giving us the English word "justification" as we read them in the Revised Standard Version of the New Testament. But since we have ventured this modest distance into Greek (and some readers, we trust, are conversant with New Testament Greek), we cannot stop without including a neighboring verse in the fifth chapter of Romans.

| Rom. 5:18 | *Dikaioma.* | The same word we found in Rom. 5:16, above. |
| | *Dikaiosis.* | Now we are back to the word used in Rom. 4:25. |

The point of these two Greek words will be understood better when seen in the text of the verse itself, which reads, "Then as one man's trespass led to condemnation for all men, so one man's act of righteousness *[dikaioma]* leads to acquittal *[dikaiosis]* and life for all men." As for the first of these, remember that above we spoke of Paul's own way of using the term—"a 'right act' in fulfilment of legal requirement."[4] Since Paul is skilfully developing the contrasts between Adam and Christ, it is plain that in this verse "one man's act of righteousness" can only be the act of Christ. Our lexicon helps us further with this comment about "the right action or conduct of Christ":

> Materially this agrees with other statements of Paul to the effect that Christ, placed under the Law (Gal. 4:4), did not merely fulfil it negatively by having no personal knowledge of sin (2 Cor. 5:21), but also positively by obedience even to death (Phil. 2:8). In Rom. 5:18 all this is gathered up in the single statement that his total life is *dikaioma*, i.e., a perfect fulfillment of the divine requirement.[5]

But there is still the other word in Rom. 5:18, *dikaiosis,* translated, as we see from the RSV, "acquittal." I made a point of underscoring part of what the lexicon said about this word, which bears a repeated quoting here: " . . . the act of justification by the divine acquittal *and with reference to the whole existence of man before God"* (Again, italics mine). We will want to make this point in other ways on later occasions, but it is well that we seize this opportunity to apply justification "to the whole existence of man before God." Justification is too often narrowly conceived, limited to man's "spiritual life," or squeezed into one brief moment of time at the instant of a man's conversion. Our aim is to present justification as a benefit extending over and throughout the entire range of your life and mine. If you are justified by the grace of God in Christ, then you are every bit as justified when you mail a letter or repair a dripping faucet as you are when you stand to hear the Gospel read in church.

In speaking in this way, we are only trying to follow the direction of Paul's thought in Romans 5:18 when he uses the two special words we have been discussing. The diagram below represents, by means of two boxes and a large arrow between them, the relationship between Christ's work on the left and the corresponding benefits received by man on the right.

Romans 5:18

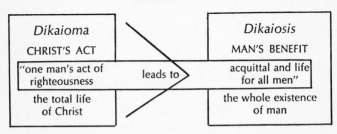

Dikaioma		*Dikaiosis*
CHRIST'S ACT		MAN'S BENEFIT
"one man's act of righteousness	leads to	acquittal and life for all men"
the total life of Christ		the whole existence of man

That is really what all theology is about—the relationship between God and what he is doing in Christ and the results of his actions in the lives of men. We learned from the Old Testament that God's righteousness is not just a static quality which he has and enjoys by himself; it is rather his willingness to act in order to vindicate his people. Now we can look at a concise New Testament statement which puts the same matter in the sharpest possible way. Rom. 3:26 gives us this sentence: " . . . It [Christ's death] was to prove at the present time that he himself is righteous *(dikaios)* and that he justifies *(dikaióo)* him who has faith in Jesus." The two transliterated Greek words provide all the commentary we need. God's *justifying* work in the death of Christ is of a piece with, consistent with, his *just* character. Again, who God is and what he does in history is shown to be the ground and source of what happens to the believer. What is God's character? He is just, righteous, *dikaios*. What does he do for man? He justifies, *dikaióo*.

God's basic character as a righteous God is shown, yes, even proved, in the fact that he justifies him who has faith in Jesus. God is not letting down the standards in justifying man! He is upholding them!

So far we have dealt with only a handful of verses where a well-known English translation of the Bible employs the noun "justification." To the original three verses we added two more, Rom. 5:18 and Rom. 3:26, where other English renderings occur. But now our study of justification must take us into the verb "to justify." A rapid count of the appearances of some form of this verb in Paul's letters produces at least twenty-three occurrences, more than we can conveniently discuss. We shall examine only some of the most important passages.

Justification in Galatians and Romans

The clearest Pauline statements on justification are to be found in the letters to the Galatians and to the Romans. Since Galatians preceded Romans in Paul's literary production, we turn first to two clusters of passages in chapters two and three of the former letter. We have already spoken about the situation reflected in Galatians 2. Paul recounts the episode in Antioch which exposed an inconsistency in the actions of Cephas (or Peter). Peter at an earlier time had extended the right hand of fellowship to Paul and Barnabas, a gesture which amounted to an endorsement of evangelistic efforts among the Gentiles. The inconsistency was that in Antioch Peter first ate with Gentiles (Gal. 2:12), but later withdrew from this symbolically important fellowship when certain men came from James, the head of the Jerusalem church.

This kind of vacillating conduct, Paul complained, meant that Peter and those whom he influenced "were not straightforward about the truth of the Gospel" (Gal. 2:14). Rebuking Peter publicly, Paul insisted, in what is a most interesting argument, that the principle of justification was made clear to Christians who were Jews by birth. It is probable that Paul is conscious of a point of view which claimed that the idea of justification was a Gentile invention and hence suspect. No, says Paul, we who are Jews by birth "know that a man is not justified by works of the law but through faith in Jesus Christ" (Gal. 2:16). He continues, making the point indisputably clear, "even we have believed in Christ Jesus, in order to be justified by faith in Christ, and not by works of the law, because by works of the law shall no one be justified."

We offer two comments on this passage. First, justification by works of the law is ruled out as being inconsistent with the Gospel; justification comes through faith in Jesus Christ. Second, as we pointed out in the first chapter, the context of this particular discussion of justification is the question of full fellowship between Jewish and Gentile Christians. Professor Nils Dahl summarizes the issue in Gal. 2 as follows: "To Paul, justification by faith is virtually denied if Jewish prerogatives of birth and patterns of behavior are made prerequisite for church fellowship, realized at the common meal."[6] Another eminent New Testament scholar has said that justification by faith is the answer to a concrete ecclesiastical problem: Jews and Gentiles. Since justification is by faith and not by works of the law, then it is senseless and wrong to perpetuate in the church the old separation between the two groups.

In our day we take for granted that the only problem Paul had in mind was the problem of how a man is saved. But he also had in mind as he wrote Galatians the practical problem of how Jews and Gentiles, both of Christian persuasion, could express the unity of the church by unrestricted fellowship with one another.

In Gal. 3 Paul introduces the figure of the Old Testament patriarch, Abraham, in order to show that the principle of justification has good precedent in antiquity. Abraham believed God, and his faith was reckoned to him as righteousness (Gal. 3:6). Furthermore, the promise to Abraham that he would be instrumental in the blessing of all nations pointed forward to the justification of the Gentiles. And all of this happened in Abraham's experience long before the law was given, so Paul's opponents were deprived of their argument that the law, by virtue of its greater originality, takes precedence over the principle of justification.

Paul is quite willing to discuss the law, as long as it is kept in its place. The law had a provisional function as our custodian until Christ came, "that we might be justified by faith" (Gal. 3:24). To believe in Christ and thus be justified, Paul argues, is to stand in continuity with the noblest Old Testament tradition, the tradition of sonship, faith, and blessing which stems from Abraham. This tradition was not overthrown by the law, because the function of the law never was that of giving life (Gal. 3:21); it was rather that of exercising a provisional custodianship over God's people until Christ came. The law performs a useful service in showing man his sinful limitations, but it does not and cannot make void God's promise to Abraham and the fulfillment of that promise in Christ Jesus.

Justification in Romans is fairly well concentrated in chapters three, four, and five. Since we are reserving space below for detailed attention to a key paragraph from chapter three, let us look now at a few verses in chapters four and five. Rom. 4 finds Paul occupied with Abraham again. He was not justified by works, so he had no boast before God (Rom. 4:2). Rather, Abraham believed God and it was reckoned to him as righteousness (4:3). One who works gets wages, not a gift. The contrast between faith and works is strong in this passage. "And to one who does not work but trusts [Greek: believes] him who justifies the ungodly, his faith is reckoned as righteousness" (4:5). The word "reckoned" here and in similar connections seems to bother many people, suggesting to them that God doesn't really go by the harsh facts in the case but instead creates a fictional state of affairs. This point will come up later for further comment, but here we can state emphatically that this reckoning has the full weight of God's own word behind it. If he reckons our faith as righteousness, then it is so.

It is also of importance to Paul that Abraham responded in faith to God's promise *before* he was circumcised, reminding us once more that Paul discusses justification in contexts where the tension between Jew and Gentile in the church is a factor. Thus Abraham can be pictured as the father of all who believe, whether circumcised or not.

In Romans, chapter five, Paul begins with the famous statement, "Therefore, since we are justified by faith, we have peace with God through our Lord Jesus Christ" (5:1). A lengthy meditation could be written on the word "peace" alone. Its Old Testament equivalent is the inexpressibly rich word *shalom,* a word held dear by Hebrew-speaking people in our own time. "Shalom is much more than personal salvation. It is at once peace, integrity, community, harmony, and justice."[7]

Shalom was Jesus' parting gift to his disciples (John 14:27); Christ Jesus "is our peace" and he came preaching peace to those far off (Gentiles) and those who were near (Jews), according to the Letter to the Ephesians (4:14, 17).

Paul clearly says in Romans 5:1 that peace with God is a benefit received by the justified believer. The emphasis is on the new state of affairs in the believer's life, not on the transition from unbelief to faith. The edge is taken off Paul's point when the verse is interpreted to mean that justification represents the end of hostility beween God and man. Such an interpretation also encourages the conception of a severely vertical, individualistic God-man transaction. Granted that coming to faith involves a new, "peaceful" relationship with God; granted that faith involves individual commitment—these are not Paul's immediate concerns in Rom. 5:1. The good news he has to share with fellow Christians is that justification opens the door to a life of *shalom*. Justification itself is not the issue; it is presupposed. The issue is the new quality of life given to the believing community.

A few verses later Paul declares that "we are now justified by his blood" (5:9). The reference to "his blood" shows that justification has its objective ground in the cross of Christ. This reminder helps us avoid the common error of making our own faith so prominent that we think of justification as having been earned by our correct mental attitude. The role of faith is that of receiving God's gift of his crucified and risen Son, Jesus Christ. "Justified by his blood" is another way of stating that the whole life of Jesus, culminating in death and resurrection, is God's provision for our being put in the right with him.

Sharpening Up the Discussion
A Study of Romans 3:21-26

We have moved somewhat rapidly across a number of passages in Galatians and Romans. We can take a little more time with a paragraph in Romans three which deserves careful attention. The passage is Rom. 3:21-26, which reads as follows:

3:21 But now the righteousness of God has been manifested apart from law, although the law and the prophets bear witness to it,

3:22 the righteousness of God through faith in Jesus Christ for all who believe. For there is no distinction;

3:23 since all have sinned and fall short of the glory of God,

3:24 they are justified by his grace as a gift, through the redemption which is in Christ Jesus,

3:25 whom God put forward as an expiation by his blood, to be received by faith. This was to show God's righteousness, because in his divine forbearance he had passed over former sins;

3:26 it was to prove at the present time that he himself is righteous and that he justifies him who has faith in Jesus.

As this study has progressed, it has offered relatively little by way of explicit definitions of justification. The purpose of such reticence has been to allow the various facets of justification to emerge from the scriptural texts, without employing the texts to argue for a given definition. We have been content so far to let the scriptural language have its say, realizing that the time would come when the wealth of biblical materials should be gathered together to arrive at more precise answers to the question, What does justification mean?

We can begin sharpening up the discussion now as we focus our attention on one significant passage of the New Testament, Rom. 3:21-26. Let us remember that Paul is *not* thinking to himself: "Now I am reaching the point in this letter where I must teach my readers the meaning of justification." Paul's theme is the good news concerning Jesus Christ. Justification is one important way of elucidating that good news. In the preceding parts of Romans, Paul has painted a fearful picture of what happens when men turn away from the Creator. Both Jews and Greeks have had their particular obligations and failings. He shows that all men are under the power of sin (Rom. 3:9), that the law, whether given by revelation to the Jews or in the conscience of the Gentiles, does not provide justification, but instead stops every mouth and makes the whole world accountable before God (Rom. 3:19-20).

The paragraph we are considering presents in concentrated fashion the heart of the Christian faith. A glance at the text discloses many of the most significant words of Christendom: righteousness, law, witness, faith, Jesus Christ, sin, glory of God, justified, grace, redemption, expiation, blood. We recognize these as weighty words, but two simple words at the beginning of the paragraph are of overwhelming importance. "But now" is a thunderclap which is still reverberating in history. These two words serve notice that a totally new age has been ushered in. There is a fresh manifestation of the righteousness of God. God has struck again! His righteousness, mentioned three times in the paragraph, is revealed, according to Rom. 1:16-17, in the Gospel. "The Gospel" is Paul's way of summing up the central event of Christ and all it means for humanity. The Gospel is not a verbal thing; it is a divine activity. The righteousness of God revealed in the Gospel is God's benevolent activity on behalf of men. We are reminded of Old Testament usages, such as, "Lead me, O Lord, in thy righteousness" (Psalm 5:8) and "in thy righteousness deliver me" (Psalm 31:1 and Psalm 71:2).

But now God's righteousness finds expression in the event of Jesus Christ. The accent is not on righteousness as a description of an attribute of God, but as divine effort to reach men. The moment in the divine schedule has been reached which was anticipated by the law and the prophets. That is, there were evidences in the history of Israel that what God was doing would one day be completed by a fresh burst of saving action. Now it has come in the form of Christ's appearance among men. This is something quite different from asserting that Jesus talked about God's righteousness and taught something new about it. Men are invited to recognize in Jesus Christ himself the arrival of the new age, the new manifestation of God's redemptive will.

Translations inevitably imply some elements of interpretation. The way Romans 3:22 is translated in the Revised Standard Version actually offers what we may call the conventional interpretation: " . . . the righteousness of God through faith in Jesus Christ for all who believe." According to this reading, the idea of faith is given twice. First comes the noun, "*faith* in Jesus Christ," then the verb, "all who *believe.*" Expressed in this way, the idea is an extremely awkward one. Instead of giving us the expected sequence—righteousness of God, Jesus Christ, faith—the RSV translation says in effect—righteousness of God, faith, faith. It makes little sense to maintain that God manifests his righteousness through our faith in Christ, and that this is done for all who believe.

A look at the Greek text will prove useful here.

Greek: *Dia pisteos Iesou Xristou*—through faith of
Jesus Christ. . . .
RSV: through faith in Jesus Christ . . .

We observe first that the Greek text does not have the
preposition "in" preceding the words "Jesus Christ."
Rather, the three words following the preposition *dia*
are all in the genitive case, which accounts for our provisional translation "through faith *of* Jesus Christ." (For
those wishing more details, when the preposition *dia*
is followed by a genitive, it means "through.") A second observation has to do with the meaning of the
noun *pisteos (pistis* in the nominative case). Does it
refer to man's faith in Jesus Christ, as RSV has it, or is
another meaning possible? The RSV itself recognizes
that *pistis* can sometimes be translated "faithfulness,"
as in Rom. 3:3: "What if some were unfaithful? Does
their faithlessness nullify the faithfulness *(pistis)* of
God?"

When we make use of "faithfulness" as a valid meaning of *pistis* in Rom. 3:22, the reading becomes, "the
righteousness of God through the faithfulness of Jesus
Christ for all who believe."[8] This translation gives us
a more logical and theological sequence: (1) righteousness of God, (2) faithfulness of Jesus Christ, (3) faith of
man. To put these three important affirmations into
different words, God's active desire to bless humanity
takes personal, historical form in the faithful career of
Jesus whose presence among men calls forth their response of trust. A simple diagram will illustrate that
the faithfulness of Jesus Christ is the bridge which connects God's righteousness on the one side and man on
the other.

Romans 3:22

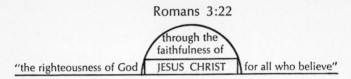

"the righteousness of God | through the faithfulness of JESUS CHRIST | for all who believe"

God is eager to display his righteousness. As Otto Piper once put it, "The problem of righteousness is not men's righteousness but God's righteousness." Paul will say in Rom. 3:26 that God even wants to prove that he is righteous. Our diagram of vs. 22 shows that God displays his righteousness, not in some general information called "Jesus Christ," but in the actual faithfulness of this Jesus in carrying out his Father's will on earth.

Our traditional preoccupation with Jesus' divinity leads us to overlook the specific substance of his earthly life. We should ask, not only, Who was he? but also, What did he do? Jesus was faithful to God in all things. The tempter offered what seemed an easier road to the fulfillment of his calling, but Jesus resisted. He was faithful in doing the will of the Father, in healing the sick, casting out demons, preaching the kingdom to the poor, and following the road of suffering to Calvary. John, the writer of Revelation, is mindful of Jesus' complete fidelity in his calling when he gives Jesus the title "the faithful witness" (Rev. 1:5). The same word, *pistos* ("faithful"), is used by Paul of God himself: "God is faithful" (1 Cor. 10:13).

As we read the Bible, the actions of God are what to look for. In the Old Testament it is the history of Israel, which is the history of God's dealings with his people. In the New Testament the main part of the story is in what Jesus does and what happens to him. Justification moves in the realm of deeds. It is in the arena of actual historical life that God makes known his righteousness. But God's way of making something known is to act. He acts decisively in the faithful life of Jesus. Man's justification takes place when, by faith, he becomes associated with Jesus Christ, the faithful one.

To continue with the examination of Rom. 3:21-26, Paul presents in verses 22 and 23 the oft-quoted statement, "For there is no distinction; since all have sinned and fall short of the glory of God . . . . " That man is a sinner, and as such one who commits actual sins, does not require further elaboration at this point. We indicated earlier that the full gravity of man's falling short of the glory of God is an important dimension of this verse.[9] It is not an afterthought tacked on to the main statement. Paul sensed man's potential greatness as the creature whose destiny it was to reflect God's glory in the world. And therefore Paul also sensed the full tragedy of man's failure to be what God intended.

There is a certain morbid way of fastening upon the sinfulness of man as a topic to be dutifully exploited, for without it, so we are led to understand, the rest of our theology will not come out right. Quite a different opinion castigates Paul for being a pessimist, not recognizing the good in man. Neither view understands Paul's thought. The first thinks that a prescribed amount of brooding about man's sinfulness is necessary to set the stage for the message of redemption. The second thinks that it is unhealthy for people to think about sin as Paul did, because men are naturally good.

Paul's grasp of man's tragic disobedience and of his high destiny goes beyond that of either critics or admirers. Man's disobedience is not tragic because a law is broken, but because his divinely appointed goal is not reached. Moreover, the drama of man's life before God

is not played out as a theological game, where the
rules require that a villainous foil be present for the
hero to vanquish. Sin and redemption are realities
too serious to become merely contrasting topics in a
neatly balanced game played by theologians.

Before leaving verse 23 we should remark that
Paul's use of "all" in the phrase "since all have
sinned" is the negative counterpart of the erasing of
all distinctions between men. That is, the revolutionary
change wrought in the world in the "but now" of
Christ's appearance opens the possibility that all men,
if they but believe, may know God's redemptive love.
It no longer matters whether one is a Jew or a Gentile.
That is the positive side of the matter. But Christ's coming also turns the light of truth on the human situation
to reveal that all men have sinned. We can endure this
disclosure of universal sin only when it comes as the
obverse side of the universal hope of redemption.

In Romans 3:24-25 Paul proceeds to the heart of his
positive statement of what constitutes the good news.
" . . . they are justified by his grace as a gift, through
the redemption which is in Christ Jesus, whom God
put forward as an expiation by his blood, to be received
by faith." Who are justified? Not all men in general.
Not all who sinned. The ones justified are "all who
believe" (vs. 22). The same factor of faith is mentioned
in 3:25, "to be received by faith."

The question of who are justified seems easily an-
swered, but even the clear statement that those who
believe in Christ are justified has to be distinguished
from two possible errors. The first is that because the
death and resurrection of Christ were indeed *for* all
men, one may assume that all mankind is justified. This
error emphasizes the objective fact of Christ's work
and its universal scope without giving full weight to

the fact that what is offered must be received. The second error looks only at the qualifying factor, faith, and from that concludes that Christ died and rose again only for believers. This view errs in failing to recognize that potentially all men may share in the salvation won by Christ. It tries to make the Gospel the exclusive possession of a restricted group. The only solution to these two recurring misconceptions is to accept the paradox that the Gospel is indeed for all men and at the same time it takes effect only among the believing.

The Gift of Grace

By placing a new heading at this point we underscore the theocentric nature of justification. It starts with God; it is God's doing. "They are justified by his grace" is a statement announcing God's love in action, for that is what grace is. God takes the initiative in the life, death, and resurrection of Jesus Christ. But more than that, God himself brings about a change in the lives of men. Grace is thus a divine movement in history, not an abstract truth about God. The Old Testament sees the grace of God as his faithfulness to the covenant which he made with his people. N. H. Snaith writes, "For Paul, the death of Christ had broken down the middle wall of partition between Jew and Gentile, with the result that all the wealth of God's covenant-love was now available for every man."[10] Justification by God's grace is therefore not a novel emergency measure; it is the execution of God's original intention.

"Justified by his grace as a gift." One Greek word, *dorean,* does duty where our Bible has "as a gift." The first implication of the phrase is that what is received from God through Christ is undeserved; it is freely bestowed upon those who are not asked to pay for it.

There is another implication. The mention of "gift" reinforces the thought of God's initiative in taking specific action on our behalf. And that specific action is Christ. Otherwise we would possess no insight beyond what the Old Testament believers had, for they too were acquainted with God's loyalty to the covenant. The New Testament announces nothing new when it declares that God is love. Millions of people accept this general fact and assume that since God is love man's condition is acceptable the way it is. To find the specifically Christian core in Paul's thought we have to go beyond general principles to the concrete act of God in Christ. A particular gift must be bestowed, and received.

"Through the redemption which is in Christ Jesus" further clarifies the event which makes justification possible. Redemption should not be thought of here as the payment of a sum of money. Paul is referring rather to the act of redemption, the liberation Christ effected for us through his ministry, death, and victorious resurrection. The Old Testament parallel is the redemption of Israel, by which we mean Israel's deliverance from Egyptian bondage. "The Lord has brought you out with a mighty hand, and redeemed you from the house of bondage, from the hand of Pharaoh king of Egypt" (Deut. 7:8). Although redemption first suggests what one is delivered from, whether bondage or sin or death, it also implies the new state of freedom which results from the liberation. As the children of Israel were redeemed in order to enjoy a new status and calling as God's chosen people, so our redemption in Christ Jesus ushers us into a new life of fellowship and service.

We have now come to Rom. 3:25 where the phrase "whom God put forward as an expiation by his blood, to be received by faith" brings to an end a sentence which began in verse 22 with the words, "For there is no distinction." To recap briefly, vs. 23 stated that all have sinned and fall short of the glory of God; vs. 24 presented the verb, "justified," and linked it with the gracious gift of God "through the redemption which is in Christ Jesus." It is rewarding to notice as we go along that Paul uses a variety of terms in describing the redemptive work of Christ. Now we come to the phrase "expiation by his blood" (vs. 25). Again, it is God who makes the first move; he "puts forward" Christ. Serious distortions of the Bible's teachings have resulted in the past from the view that salvation takes place by having Jesus step between man and an angry God who has to be placated. But Paul teaches us that God and his Son are working together, not against one another. "Christ Jesus, whom God put forward." Another important statement to the same effect is 2 Cor. 5:19, "God was in Christ reconciling the world to himself."

"Expiation by his blood" is admittedly a difficult expression. Jesus Christ has to be both God's way to man and man's way to God, never just one of these. So from God's side there is the putting forward of Christ, as we have just seen. From man's side, Jesus Christ, the perfect man, shows his willingness to give up his life for our salvation. Bound together in the life and actions of the Son of God are the divine mercy which desires our salvation and the human willingness to acknowledge God as God. From Jesus' willingness to honor and obey God comes the offer of a pleasing sacrifice—the giving up of his whole life in faithful, loving obedience to his God-given calling.

Those who do not understand the biblical meaning of sacrifice find "expiation by his blood" quite against their liking. The common mistake is to assume that sacrifice is a primitive method of buying off an angry God, but the Old Testament has a very different interpretation of it. God himself provided a system of sacrifices in order that sinful man, who had forfeited his life by his misdeeds, could substitute something else for his life. For such a sacrifice to be pleasing to God it had to be given in the attitude that acknowledged the sin and repented of it. In other words, the Old Testament sacrifices were not to be offered in an indifferent, mechanical way; they were offered rather as the visible sign that the offender had repented. That is exactly what Psalm 51 means when it speaks of the broken and contrite heart of the person bringing his offering. At first glance, the reader of this Psalm might think that God no longer wanted any actual sacrifices, only a broken spirit. But as one reads the rest of the Psalm it is plain that sacrifices and burnt offerings continue to be given—and received—after the penitent has been cleansed of his sin (Psalm 51:18-19).

It is against this Old Testament background that Paul uses the expression "expiation by his blood." We know that "to expiate" means "to atone for, to appease, to make amends," but we also know that this sacrificial language constitutes only one set of the images used by Paul. There has also been the language of redemption from slavery and the language of justification. The main point is that Christ is God's act of atonement, the means he employs to bring man back into the right relationship with himself. Therefore we have to see Christ's sacrifice as the event in which God is at work; at the same time we have to see how serious is the plight of man that such a drastic remedy was necessary.

Rightly understood, there is a sense in which Christ's

death on the cross is pleasing to God. Not because God takes pleasure in Jesus' sufferings. That which God finds pleasing is Jesus' obedient willingness to give up his life for us and in so doing to give God the whole-hearted response of obedience and faith which the whole human race was expected to give. Too often we think of Christ as our substitute without remembering that by faith we are identified with him in his death. We may use an even stronger word: we are incorporated into Christ. Thus when the Representative Man dies, we die. We are allowed to share in that faith and obedience which Christ showed in life and in death. But if our hearts remain unchanged, if we do not receive Christ by faith, then his work is still of no benefit to us. Christ is put forward as a means of atonement, says Paul, "to be received by faith."

The word "blood" requires another note of explanation. Why is blood so important? Not because of its magical properties, but because it is the ultimate symbol of *life*. Unfortunately, our theology sometimes reverses this in such a way that "blood" serves only to symbolize the death of Christ. The words of J. S. Whale are instructive in this connection. "Sacrifice is gravely misinterpreted when its meaning is limited to the death of the victim. Thus to isolate one element in the ritual is to misconceive its purpose, which is not the destruction of life but the representative surrender of life. This is the God-given way whereby the sinner identifies himself with the life offered to God."[11] In the case of Jesus Christ, the supreme sacrifice, his death has expiatory power because it signifies that his entire life — birth, public ministry, passion, resurrection, exaltation — is what God finds pleasing. To believe in Jesus is not to entertain somber thoughts about the moment of his crucifixion; it is to rejoice that in baptism we have been incorporated into his whole life.

Next Paul returns to the theme of God's righteousness (3:25b): "This was to show God's righteousness . . . . " Man by nature mistrusts God. To hear that God is righteous only strengthens the impulse to flee from God, as was the case, for example, in the mind of Martin Luther. The reason for this tendency is twofold. Man senses his unworthiness, which causes him to feel guilty. Secondly, most men regard God's righteousness only as his determination to punish sin. But the Gospel offers a surprise. It declares that God's righteousness is actually a reaching out for man, not a rejection of man. Now, says Paul, the sending of Jesus Christ into the world was intended to convince the world that the righteous God cares for men, despite the guilt of sin, and that God is not stepping out of character when he does this. Quite the contrary. It is in the putting forward of Christ that God finally and fully discloses his character!

"This was to show God's righteousness, because in his divine forbearance he had passed over former sins." We have already commented on the first part of this sentence. As to the second part, God's passing over of former sins, we need only observe that Paul thinks that the divine forbearance raised a question concerning God's righteousness, requiring now the vindication of his righteousness.[12] Going on to verse 26, the final verse in the paragraph, we read, "it was to prove at the present time that he himself is righteous and that he justifies him who has faith in Jesus." It is striking that at the beginning and the end of this argument Paul stresses the present tense significance of Christ's work: "but now" in verse 21 and "at the present time" in verse 26. Our inclination is to consign God to the past. God acted back then, we say, in Moses' or David's time. Paul believed in a God who did new things.

Something new and incomparable faces us in this verse when Paul declares that God is proving his righteousness as he justifies. Against the conventional idea that God's true character was revealed when he gave the law at Mt. Sinai, we have learned from Paul that it is in Jesus Christ that God discloses his essential character. The challenge of faith is to overcome the fixation that Christ, grace, forgiveness, and acceptance are all departures by the Almighty from his regular norm. But there is a further thought here, one which is seldom discussed. God does his saving work in public, submitting his actions to man's scrutiny, inviting man to examine and weigh the divine activity in history in order to see that it is just! God is thus justifying himself as he justifies man!

This bold idea goes beyond anything in the earlier stages of revelation. It may remind us that the Old Testament Book of Job voices the complaint that God doesn't allow anyone to get a hearing with him.

> Oh, that I knew where I might find him, that I might come even to his seat! I would lay my case before him and fill my mouth with arguments. I would learn what he would answer me, and understand what he would say to me. . . . There an upright man could reason with him, and I should be acquitted for ever by my judge (Job 23:3-6, 7; cf. Job 9).

We read the entire story of Job's agonizing over the question of God's justice, finally to discover no resolution other than Job's submission to God through a deeper apprehension of God as one whose purposes cannot be thwarted (Job 42:2).

But here, at the heart of the New Testament, Paul offers the insight that God is willing to lay his justice on the line. Instead of remaining aloof and inscrutable, God in Christ enters the lists to prove that he is righteous. We note again the striking correspondence between God's character and his activity. He proves "at the present time that he himself is righteous *[dikaios]* and that he justifies *[dikaiounta]* him who has faith in Jesus" (Rom. 3:26). What God is corresponds to his justifying activity.

To conclude our examination of Rom. 3:21-26, let us put the entire argument in somewhat more familiar language. The greatest moment in human history has arrived in the coming of Christ. The content of this decisive moment is the disclosure of God's liberating and restoring power. The mode of the disclosure is the faithful life of Jesus on earth which is meant to persuade men that they may have confidence in God. He brings to completion what he began centuries ago. Now men are asked to identify themselves with Christ, the historical embodiment of God's purpose. The invitation is to all, without distinction, for all stand on the common ground of having sinned and missed their true destiny.

The work of Christ is described in images of acquittal, liberation, and sacrifice. The believing man is vindicated, his life endorsed by divine verdict. He is delivered from enslavement. His guilt is removed through the offering of Jesus' life. All of this announces God's righteousness to the world. God is consistent with himself and his plans for the whole human race. To believe in Jesus Christ is to stake one's life that God is executing his redemptive plan in this particular way, through the cross and resurrection of Christ. This particular message does not mention the resurrection, we may note, but Rom. 4:25 clearly associates resurrection with justification. As we indicated earlier, the entire life of Jesus constitutes his faithfulness, not just the moment of his death. To put the resurrection in the right perspective we may say that it displays God's faithfulness. By raising Jesus from the dead, God places his seal of approval upon the faithful life which Jesus offered up in death.

The point of strongest emphasis in Rom. 3:21-26 is the demonstration of God's righteousness in the faithfulness of Christ. As C. K. Barrett points out, a demonstration in this sense means "both a simple showing forth, and also a proof, effected by showing forth."[13] The greatness of this decisive deed at this turning point in history so dominates Paul's mind in this text that the human experience of justification has to be inferred from the words "believe" and "faith."

Looking back over all the Pauline texts we have discussed, we note that the same general observation holds: Paul places great weight on the historical, Christ-centered *basis* of justification, being less precise in describing what justification signifies in the life of the believer. Nevertheless, the human side of justification takes on substance when we list the terms and associations which surround Paul's discussion:

JUSTIFICATION . . .

    means full fellowship among Christians
                       Gal. 2:14-16
    by faith in Christ and not by works of the law
                       (Gal. 2:16)
    is in harmony with the grace of God
                       (Gal. 2:21; Rom. 3:24)
    is the opposite of condemnation (Rom. 5:16)
    means acquittal and life for all men (Rom. 5:18)
    implies the forgiveness of sins
                       (Rom. 3:23-24; 5:8-9)

opens the way to peace with God (Rom. 5:1)
declares that faith is reckoned as righteousness
                                    (Rom. 4:5)
has an eschatological dimension
                                    (Gal. 5:5, see ch. IV)

It remains for later theologians and teachers to weave these Pauline materials into doctrines of justification. We end the chapter by noting that the chapter title, "Everyone Can Be Justified," turns out to be a very accurate summary of Paul's treatment of justification. It is for everyone because it is God's work, because all men need it, because Christ as the second Adam is the man for all, and because all can believe.

3.

Churchmen Interpret Justification

The study of justification begins with the Bible, especially the New Testament, as authoritative teaching. In addition, it is profitable to consult the interpretations of skilled Christian teachers, past and present. This chapter will examine several excerpts from the writings of Martin Luther, the reformer whose insights into the meaning of justification continue to enrich the church. After dealing with Luther and his successors we will move quickly to modern times where we discover that *Justification Today* is the theme of an important pamphlet published in 1965 by the Lutheran World Federation.

Learning from Luther

Two things about Luther's rediscovery of justification stand out at once. First, justification became for him an experienced reality, and a "teaching" only secondarily. Therefore, to learn from Luther we must examine what he says about this experience. A second feature in Luther's fresh outlook on justification is that the starting point is the struggle to understand "the righteousness of God." The latter idea was very prominent in Paul's thought, as we saw in the previous chapter.

The word "justice" (Latin: *justitia*) comes into the discussion again because the Bible used by Luther read "Justitia Dei" (Justice of God) where we find "righteousness of God." The problem of God's righteousness came up as Luther prepared lectures on the Book of Psalms. Of inestimable importance is Luther's reflection on the opening of Psalm 22, which became Jesus' cry from the cross, "My God, my God, why hast thou forsaken me?" If the innocent Christ could utter such a cry, it could only mean that he too knew what it was to experience terror and alienation from God. It dawned on Luther that his own severe *Anfechtungen* (assaults, temptations, sufferings) were not unknown to the very Son of God himself. The Christ whom medieval piety was fond of picturing as the stern, forbidding Judge[1] was now seen to be one who on the cross tasted the suffering of desolation and abandonment, not only at the hands of men, but from the presence of the Almighty. How could this be explained other than by Christ's submission of himself to the lot of the sinner? "He who was without sin for our sakes became sin and so identified himself with us as to participate in our alienation."[2]

Further light came from this phrase: " . . . in thy righteousness deliver me" (Psalm 31:1). The synonym "justice" in place of "righteousness" emphasizes why Luther was so amazed to see the connection between justice and deliverance. It is the God of justice to whom the psalmist prays for deliverance. "The connection of righteousness [or justice] and deliverance challenged the conception that the former always meant the demanding, judicial, fearful justice of God," write two American interpreters, Dillenberger and Welch.[3]

We are unusually fortunate in having access to autobiographical material in which Luther relates how he

finally came to an understanding—and experience—
of what the apostle Paul means by the "justice" of
God in the first chapter of Romans. The extensive
passage cited below is presented as cited in Gordon
Rupp's book *The Righteousness of God*. The reader
will find a slightly different translation of the passage
in *Here I Stand,* the well-known biography of Luther by
the Yale church historian Roland Bainton.[4]

Meanwhile then, in that year (1519), I turned once
more to interpret the Psalms, relying on the fact
that I was the more expert after I had handled in
the schools the letter of St. Paul to the Romans
and the Galatians, and that which is to the Hebrews.
Certainly I had been seized with a greater ardour to
understand Paul in the Epistle to the Romans, but
as Virgil says, it was not "coldness of the blood."
which held me up until now, but one word that is,
chapter 1. "The Justice of God is revealed in it"
(Justitia Dei). For I hated this word "Justitia Dei"
which by the use and consent of all doctors I was
taught to understand philosophically of that formal
or active justice (as they call it) with which God is
just, and punishes unjust sinners.

For, however irreproachably I lived as a monk, I
felt myself in the presence of God to be a sinner
with a most unquiet conscience nor could I trust
that I had pleased him with my satisfaction. I did
not love, nay, rather I hated this just God who
punished sinners and if not with "open blasphemy"
certainly with huge murmuring I was angry with
God, saying: "As though it really were not enough
that miserable sinners should be eternally damned
with original sin, and have all kinds of calamities
laid upon them by the law ·of the ten commandments, God must go and add sorrow upon sorrow
and even through the Gospel itself bring his Justice
and his Wrath to bear!" I raged in this way with a
fierce and disturbed conscience, and yet I knocked

importunately at Paul in this place, thirsting most ardently to know what St. Paul meant.

At last, God being merciful, as I meditated day and night on the connection of the words, namely, the Justice of God is revealed in it, as it is written, " 'the Just shall live by Faith,' " there I began to understand the Justice of God as that by which the just lives by the gift of God, namely by faith, and this sentence, "the Justice of God is revealed in the gospel," to be that passive justice, with which the merciful God justifies us, by faith, as it is written "The just lives by faith."

This straightway made me feel as though reborn, and as though I had entered through open gates into paradise itself. From then on, the whole face of scripture appeared different. I ran through the scriptures then, as memory served, and found the same analogy in other words, as the Work of God (opus) that which God works in us, Power of God (virtus Dei) with which he makes us strong, wisdom of God (sapientia Dei) with which he makes us wise, fortitude of God, salvation of God, glory of God.

And now, as much as I had hated this word "Justice of God" before, so much the more sweetly I extolled this word to myself now, so that this place in Paul was to me as a real gate of paradise. Afterwards, I read Augustine, "On the Spirit and the Letter," where beyond hope I found that he also similarly interpreted the Justice of God: that with which God endues us, when he justifies us. . . . Armed with these cogitations I began to interpret the Psalms again.[5]

To offer comment on such a moving account of a decisive personal experience almost seems superfluous. At the same time, it is not out of place to do some analyzing because the episode itself combined an overpowering emotion with a careful exercise of the mind. "I meditated day and night on the connection of the words," Luther says, or, as the German historian Heinrich Boehmer reports the matter, "he hit upon the idea of examining the context more carefully."[6] In his passionate desire to understand Paul, Luther summoned his energies to the humble, painstaking work of examining the text of Scripture. Insight into justification did not come because Luther's emotions were aroused; it came because he thirsted for understanding enough to drive himself to study words, sentences, grammar, and contexts. But what, specifically, was the insight into justification?

That justification is not by works but by faith? Such an answer threatens to reduce the significance of a momentous experience to a slogan. The insight is basically the discovery of the meaning of God's righteousness. "I began to understand the Justice of God as that by which the just lives by the gift of God, namely by faith, . . . justice, with which the merciful God justifies us, by faith, as it is written 'The just lives by faith.' " Rather than continuing to repel him as "that formal or active justice (as they call it) with which God is just, and punishes unjust sinners," God's righteousness was now seen by Luther as that gracious activity of God in Christ, revealed in the Gospel, whereby God gives and saves and shows mercy.

In a comment on Rom. 3:7 Luther speaks of three ways in which the righteousness of God is shown: first, when in his punishment of the unjust he causes human injustice to witness to his righteousness; second, when human injustice is compared to his righteousness, making the latter appear beautiful in comparison; third, when God justifies us. Luther illustrates the three ways by comparing God to a master craftsman. He may criticize the bungling efforts of the

apprentices, he may set his fine workmanship along-
side theirs, but best of all, he may impart his own
skills to them so they too will become skilled in the
mysteries of the craft.[7]

The insight into the meaning of righteousness is a
lightning flash which illumines the very nature of
God and his saving work. In gathering up several similar expressions, such as work of God, power of God,
and wisdom of God, Luther shows how his eyes were
opened to an especially important feature of Scripture. These phrases are not merely labels for various
qualities or attributes of God; they are witnesses to
God's actions! Luther cited the fifth-century thinker
Augustine as one who "similarly interpreted the Justice
of God." A rather complex story lies back of Luther's
modification of older interpretations,[8] but something
he learned from Augustine is apparent right at this
point: that which Scripture declares concerning God is
disclosed in Jesus Christ, and further, that which is
revealed in and through Christ finds its correspondence
in the life of believing man. In other words, Luther
learned from reading Augustine that in Scripture there
is a parallel between theological statements (what is
said about God) and psychological statements (how
man is affected).[9] This is true because the Holy Spirit
opens the mind of the believer to the meaning of
Scripture. With this principle in mind, let us summar-
ize what Luther has been telling us:

Scripture speaks of	THE JUSTICE OF GOD
Disclosed historically in	THE GOSPEL OF JESUS CHRIST
Realized by the believer in	FAITH IN CHRIST

Notice how the pivotal element is Jesus Christ.
Without the middle step we would be forced to speak

of God and his righteousness without reference to anything that has happened in history. For Luther it was all-important that the righteousness of God was "revealed in the Gospel" (Rom. 1:17), that is, in Jesus Christ. Christianity declares that God showed his righteousness in sending Christ to the world. In heeding and receiving the good news about Jesus Christ, his life, death, and resurrection, men receive Christ himself and in that very step of faith they are justified.

Sometimes well-informed Christians heedlessly lapse into the use of general theological statements which prove to be empty of any reference to Christ and his work of redemption. Against such carelessness in reference to justification, Luther has some blunt but instructive words in a comment on Rom. 5:2, "Through him we have obtained access to this grace in which we stand":

> He [Paul] speaks against those presumptuous persons who think they can come to God apart from Christ, as though it were sufficient for them to have believed, and thus "sola fide" not through Christ (per Christum) but alongside Christ (juxta Christum) or beyond Christ, not needing him having once accepted the grace of justification . . . but it is necessary to have Christ always, hitherto and to eternity as mediator of such faith. . . . [10]

There is a natural order in Luther's talk about justification. First, the meaning of the righteousness of God; second, the central place of Christ; third, the nature of faith. Before proceeding to some remarks about faith, let us observe what students of Luther are rightly fond of pointing out—that the experience of justification means the exchange of the believing man's sin for the righteousness of Christ. Luther writes:

> Whence, then, is our defence? Nowhere save from
> Christ and in Christ. For if there shall come some
> reproach against the heart which believes in Christ,
> testifying against him concerning some evil deed,
> then it turns itself away, and turns to Christ and
> says—"But he made satisfaction. He is the Righteous
> One," this is my defence. He cried for me, he made
> his Righteousness to be mine, and made my sin
> his own, and if he made my sin his own, then I can
> have it now no longer, and I am free. And if he has
> made his Righteousness mine, I am righteous with
> the same Righteousness as his.[11]

Now it is time to speak about faith. Medieval theologians (from about the eleventh to the thirteenth century) thought of faith as assent: man assents to the doctrines of the church. It was necessary for this assent to be formed by love if it were to be a saving faith, which gives us the famous medieval phrase, "faith formed by love." This scheme required that human merit play a role in forming faith by love. Essentially, faith was still thought of as assent by the scholars. For Luther, though, faith was personal trust in God but not excluding the need to believe what the creed taught.[12]

Luther's famous treatise on good works says about faith: "And this faith, faithfulness, confidence deep in the heart, is the true fulfilling of the First Commandment."[13] Scholars have taken special note of the fact that Luther's rediscovery of the Gospel had a close connection with the First Commandment, "Thou shalt have no other gods before me" (Ex. 20:3).[14] Many readers will instinctively recite to themselves from Luther's Small Catechism, "What is meant by this Commandment?" The answer is, "We should fear, love, and trust in God above all things."[15] Luther goes on to say in the treatise on good works:

> And as this Commandment is the very first, highest
> and best, from which all the others proceed, in
> which they exist, and by which they are directed
> and measured, so also its work, that is, the faith
> or confidence in God's favor at all times, is the very
> first, highest and best, from which all others must
> proceed, exist, remain, be directed and measured.[16]

Faith is personal trust and confidence in God. It ful-
fills the First Commandment because it acknowledges
that God is God, signifying the creature's recognition
of the Creator who says, "I am the Lord thy God" (Ex.
20:2). Faith is not merely assent to Christian doctrine.
Neither is it a quality or virtue of man. How does faith
come into being? We may turn to the treatise on good
works again for Luther's answer:

> But if you ask, where the faith and the confidence
> can be found and whence they come, this it is cer-
> tainly most necessary to know. First: Without doubt
> faith does not come from your works or merit, but
> alone from Jesus Christ, and is freely promised
> and given. . . . Faith, therefore, does not begin
> with works, neither do they create it, but it must
> spring up and flow from the blood, wounds and
> death of Christ. If thou see in these that God is so
> kindly affectioned toward thee that He gives even
> His Son for thee, then thy heart also must in its
> turn grow sweet and kindly affectioned toward God,
> and so thy confidence must grow out of pure good-
> will and love—God's love toward thee and thine
> toward God.[17]

Our pastors and teachers consistently urge us to believe in Christ. They also remind us that faith is not our
own doing, it is a gift of God (Eph. 2:8). Perhaps the
point at which much preaching and teaching fall short
is in showing the relationship between the presentation of the Gospel, on the one hand, and the origin of

faith, on the other. Here is where Luther's statement
above can help us: "If thou see in these that God is so
kindly affectioned toward thee that He gives even His
Son for thee, then thy heart also must in its turn grow
sweet and kindly affectioned toward God. . . . " If, as
we say repeatedly, faith is a response to God's deed in
Christ, that means that the proclamation of that deed
exercises a moving, drawing power upon us. Faith is
born when a man is effectively faced with the reality of
Christ's life and work. We believe when Christ's cross
and resurrection persuade us that it is safe and right
to put our trust in the God who loves us to this extent!

One of the many places where Luther affirms this
same need for faith to be a personal experience of
Christ is in his *Treatise on Christian Liberty:*

> It is not enough nor is it Christian, to preach the
> works, life and words of Christ as historical facts,
> as if knowledge of these would suffice for the con-
> duct of life. . . . Rather ought Christ to be preached
> *to the end that faith in Him may be established,*
> *that He may not only be Christ but be Christ for*
> *thee and for me,* and that what is said of Him and
> what His Name denotes *may be effectual in us.*[18]

This essential lesson will deliver us from the false
notion that "to believe" is the same as mentally ac-
cepting the teachings of the Bible and church. Moreover, it warns us not to think of justification by faith as
a transaction taking place outside of man and involv-
ing him only as one who receives information that his
status has been changed.

The Holy Spirit is active in justification, as Regin
Prenter, the contemporary Danish theologian, indicates,
uniting human experience with the facts of the Gospel

story "that what is said of Him and what His Name de-
notes may be effectual in us."

One of the controversial aspects of Luther's teaching of justification by faith is his insertion of the word
"only" (Latin: *solum*) in his translation of Rom. 3:28.
This exercise of the translator's freedom has disturbed
many people, especially Roman Catholics. The verse in
question reads as follows: "For we hold that a man is
justified by faith apart from works of law" (Rom. 3:28).
In 1530 Luther wrote *On Translating: An Open Letter*,
in which he answers the critics who had objected that
the word "only" is not in the text of Romans. Luther
translated the verse: "We hold that man is justified
without the works of the law, only by faith."[19] He answers the objections with two reasons. First, the nature
of the German language demands the addition of
"only." "I wanted to speak German, not Latin or Greek,
since I had undertaken to speak German in the translation. But it is the nature of our German language that
in speaking of two things, one of which is admitted and
the other denied, we use the word 'only' along with
the word 'not' or 'no.' So we say, 'The farmer brings
only grain and no money.' "[20]

The second reason is that the subject matter discussed by Paul in Rom. 3 demands the use of "only."
Nothing is to be allowed to obscure the purity of justification by faith in Christ. Luther writes:

> Now, however, I was not only relying on the na-
> ture of the languages and following that when, in
> Romans 3, I inserted the word *solum*, "only," but
> the text itself and the sense of St. Paul demanded
> it and forced it upon me. He is dealing, in that
> passage, with the main point of Christian doctrine,
> viz., that we are justified by faith in Christ, without
> any works of the law, and he cuts away all works

so completely, as even to say that the works of
the law, though it is God's law and His Word, do
not help us to righteousness.[21]

So instead of backing down and apologizing for a
textual error, Luther forcefully and confidently affirms
the correctness of translating the verse by adding the
word "only." He knows German that well and he
claims to know Paul's intention that well. Luther's freedom at this point has caused dispute, of course, but
we know exactly on what grounds he inserted the
"only."

What he says about justification as being "the main
point of Christian doctrine" is stirring up more discussion today than the issue of adding a word to Rom.
3:28. For the most part, Lutherans have agreed that
justification is the main point in Christian teaching.
Whatever our own view might be, it is worth while to
raise such a question. This is true of any major Christian doctrine. Even if one finds himself returning to the
commonly accepted position, he has had the healthy
experience of learning for himself why he wants to
hold it. The other possibility should not be ruled out.
How else can the church continually reform itself?

Luther's Successors and Justification

Many of us might experience a momentary surprise at the omission of any extended reference to Luther's Small and Large Catechisms in the preceding section until we recall, as the English Congregationalist
J. S. Whale points out, that justification by faith alone
is not mentioned in either of those famous catechisms.[22] In reminding us of this, Whale makes an important point: Luther and the other reformers were

not bringing forth a new doctrine when they fought for the principle of faith alone, but a new standpoint. The primary article of belief for Protestants and Catholics alike, says Whale, is the atoning death and redeeming victory of the incarnate Son of God. "Luther insisted that it be taken seriously by being *believed*. He did not regard the work of Christ as one doctrine and justification by faith as another: they were the objective and subjective aspects of one and the same truth."[23] One should keep this in mind when taking up the question as to whether justification by faith is the main doctrine in Paul or in the New Testament and Christianity generally.

Even though he did not write about justification in his catechisms, Luther left his successors a great deal to ponder, as our samplings from his writings have shown. The church returns to Luther's words in order to learn from a remarkably gifted teacher who saw clearly and wrote powerfully about primary theological matters. This motive governs the study of the writings of many other teachers, to be sure. In Luther's case, we face the particular necessity of distinguishing what he taught from interpretations developed by his successors. Where Luther's description of justification by faith grew out of a profound, living experience, the view that dominated the next century made of justification a closely reasoned doctrine. As Reinhold Niebuhr writes in a recent essay, "The early Reformation protested in the name of grace against legalism. Yet by the seventeenth century this came to mean that we are saved not only 'by faith' but by '*true* faith." This meant 'faith' as 'belief,' belief in the symbolic affirmations of Lutheranism, in short, belief in the Augsburg Confession."[24]

Philip Melanchthon, Luther's close friend and colleague, was the chief architect of the *Augsburg Confession,* the main summary of Lutheran beliefs, presented to the emperor, Charles V, at the Diet of Augsburg in 1530. Article IV of the confession says this about justification: "Also they teach that men cannot be justified before God by their own strength, merits, or works, but are freely justified for Christ's sake, through faith, when they believe that they are received into favor and that their sins are forgiven for Christ's sake, who, by His death, has made satisfaction for our sins. This faith God imputes for righteousness in His sight. Rom. 3 and 4."[25] There is a suggestion here that faith has an intellectual character; man believes *that* such and such is true rather than believing *in* the God who gives us promises which we believe because we have come to trust him through Christ.

Melanchthon was gifted in the direction of logical thought and systematic presentation of ideas, for which Luther greatly admired him. But whereas faith for Luther was the commitment of the whole man in confidence to God, faith for Melanchthon was assent to what the Bible says about Christ.[26] Justification was also interpreted in an intellectual way: man learns from the Gospel the truth that Christ's work has objective validity for him.[27] Many would not agree with this criticism, especially as it pertains to Article IV of the *Augsburg Confession.* The church historian Williston Walker writes that "justification by faith is admirably defined" in this article.[28] We are all aware that the *Augsburg Confession* has served the church well for centuries. Nevertheless, insofar as faith is construed as a mental act rather than a trusting commitment of the whole person, the weakness of Article IV has to be acknowledged.

Modern Christians are understandably impatient with

the complexity and passion of the theological debates of past generations. Furthermore, it takes an expert to follow the thread of those many stormy controversies. Our more limited aim is to gain at least a general picture of what was happening to the teaching of justification by faith. At the outset it is clear that a very important Lutheran document, the Formula of Concord of 1580, reaffirms what both Luther and Melanchthon taught, namely, that justification "is the chief article in the entire Christian doctrine, without which no poor conscience can have any firm consolation, or can truly know the riches of the grace of Christ, as Dr. Luther also has written: If this only article remains pure on the battlefield, the Christian Church also remains pure."[29]

The thought expressed above gave rise to the famous phrase which has been employed a great deal by scholars: Justification is that article of faith by which the church either stands or falls. Lutherans as a whole have been convinced that justification *is* the most important teaching in Christianity, though the question has been raised anew recently, e.g., at the World Assembly of the Lutheran World Federation at Helsinki in 1963.

We have expressed some reservations about the way in which Philip Melanchthon expressed the meaning of justification by faith. We should note, however, that Melanchthon was in trouble with his fellow theologians on two other important matters. The charges were that Melanchthon was too conciliatory toward Roman Catholics and toward the Calvinists, on the one hand, and that he was guilty of teaching synergism, the cooperation of the human will in conversion, on the other hand. Students of this period of church history often credit a Lutheran scholar named Martin

Chemnitz, a pupil of Melanchthon, with an influence through teaching and writing which repudiated those points ("unionism" and "synergism") where Melanchthon was straying from Luther's position. Chemnitz had a major role in the writing of the Formula of Concord of 1580. Of this document Professor J. Pelikan writes: "The Formula achieved the cleansing of Lutheranism from the false and erroristic teachings of Philip Melanchthon, and this was the work of Chemnitz."[30]

Salutary as this cleansing was, there lingered on in Lutheran theology a spirit and an attitude, inherited from Melanchthon, which gave a rational, philosophical turn to the manner in which biblical truths were taught. Melanchthon's view of faith as a movement of the intellect and justification by faith as the acknowledgment of Scripture's promise "as certain and true" give an idea of the direction in which theology would move in the century or so after the Formula of Concord, despite that Formula's rejection of certain of Melanchthon's errors. It was a case of refuting Melanchthon's conclusions, but holding on to the methods whereby he reached his conclusions. In other words, theology was becoming a kind of philosophy, a system of logical thought which concerned itself with formulating correct doctrines. Motivated by an honest desire to follow Luther's lead, later theologians actually toned down much of his teaching. For example, Luther had a strong consciousness of sin as personal rebellion against a personal God, but a century later orthodox theologians were interpreting sin as a violation of the law.[31] Of course, sin is a transgression of the law, but primarily it is an offense against God himself, whose personal will is expressed in the law.

It is not our task to account for the revisions of Luther's theology by reviewing the many historical factors involved. We simply note that through a gradual and largely unconscious process, a view of justification emerges which uses all the proper biblical phrases but comes to be a set piece of correct doctrine rather than a vital experience.

Orthodoxy and Pietism

In speaking or writing about developments taking place in Christian thought between the days of Luther and the Reformation (16th century) and our own time, we have recourse to a set of well-used labels which characterize successive epochs in time and indicate the general theological outlook of that period. One of these labels is the word *Reformation* itself. It reminds us of the spiritual ferment of the sixteenth century, including Luther's own inner development, the memorable historical events of the posting of the Ninety-five Theses in 1517, the Augsburg Confession of 1530, the final break with Roman Catholicism, and the spread of Reformation teaching. *Orthodoxy* is a useful historical term, referring to a movement traceable within Lutheran and Calvinist churches from the late sixteenth into the early eighteenth century. The aim of Lutheran Orthodoxy was to consolidate the Lutheran heritage of the Reformation through pure doctrine. The Formula of Concord of 1580 is the first major document of Orthodoxy. The seventeenth century was the flourishing period for Orthodoxy.[32]

Pietism made its appearance in the seventeenth century but was most influential in the eighteenth century. This movement actually had roots in orthodox theology, with which it is often contrasted, but its parentage also includes pre-Reformation mystical piety.

Pietism stressed the practical, devotional life, Bible reading, laymen's participation in these activities, and the training of pastors in preaching and in devotional exercises.[33] *Rationalism* serves to indicate the type of influence at work in theology and the church in the eighteenth century when the whole cultural and intellectual milieu was characterized by the comprehensive term "Enlightenment." In an age of Enlightenment many wanted to enlighten Christian theology by elevating the role of human reason in arriving at what the church should believe and teach.

Our question is and has been: How has justification been understood and taught since the Reformation led by Luther? According to a summary offered by Hjalmar Lindroth, a Swedish scholar, justification includes two things which Luther always kept together as a unity: (1) imputation, that is, the reckoning of Christ's righteousness to us, and (2) regeneration, that is, the receiving through faith of a new, clean heart. Moreover, writes Lindroth, faith for Luther was not merely holding a doctrine to be true or a confidence in God's grace but ultimately Christ's presence with man. Melanchthon's teaching broke the unity between these two. For him, justification was an objective, divine act which God took care of in heaven, declaring man righteous, while regeneration or renewal appeared as something separate, taking place in the Christian life. In other words, Melanchthon's view was that justification is essentially imputation, a declaration of God in the courts, as it were, from which we get the idea of *forensic* or legal justification.[34]

Orthodoxy followed Melanchthon, not Luther, in its teaching of justification.[35] Thanks to the industrious and discerning research into Luther's writings which has blossomed in the present century, we are able to cor-

rect some of Orthodoxy's claims that it faithfully repre-
sented the great reformer's teachings. As we saw
earlier, some of Melanchthon's errors were indeed
recognized and repudiated, but not his general conviction that theological ideas should be placed within
a philosophical, intellectualistic frame.[36]

Let us be clear that these are not matters confined
to the scholar's study and to textbooks. The Saturday
confirmation instruction and the Sunday sermon will
be affected decisively if the pastor succeeds in distinguishing those elements in our "orthodox" tradition which vigorously echo Luther's clear, Gospel-
based teaching from those which fall below it. The
layman can appreciate that modern Lutheran theology
seeks to go back beyond a traditional Lutheran understanding of justification largely constructed by Melanchthon to Luther's own view which, in Lindroth's
words, "constitutes a hitherto unsurpassed interpretation of the Gospel."[37]

Did Pietism improve on Orthodoxy's understanding
of justification? A mixed answer has to be given. Pietism wanted to relate justification more closely to the
personal life of the believer; it was not satisfied with
the notion of an objective declaration issued in the
heavenly court. Justification should also bring about a
difference in the individual's life. Therefore Pietism
made justification one of the elements in conversion.
To use Lindroth's terminology, regeneration and renewal, the gift of a new heart through faith—these ex-
periential aspects of justification appealed to Pietism.

With its greater interest in the subjective side of
justification, Pietism ran the risk of becoming too pre-
occupied with human feelings and the outward mani-
festations of the new life in Christ. Its protest against
Orthodoxy's doctrinal formalism was legitimate; its

own efforts to restate justification in more biblical terms were only partially successful since the doing of theology was not Pietism's strong point.

Whereas Orthodoxy and Pietism were first cousins within the same family, Rationalism brought more outside influence to bear on Christian theology. The Enlightenment found its basis for interpreting human experience in man's independent reason. All of the church's assumptions regarding God, sin, salvation, and eternal life were to be tested, it was said, according to scientific standards. That this was unsettling to church people is only what we should expect, since in our day, too, Christians (including theologians) find it hard to understand the relation between faith and reason. In the eighteenth-century situation, those who sought to accommodate Rationalism to Christian thought reduced justification to a matter of moral improvement, forgiveness became God's kindly indulgence, and righteousness was viewed as a reasonable standard of decency.[38]

We are not to conclude that Rationalism succeeded in eliminating all vital Bible-based theology and with it the evangelical view of justification. Both Orthodoxy and Pietism revived in the nineteenth century, and in that same century the concerns of Rationalism gave impetus to a flowering of historical research which many tradition-minded theologians entered into. There was restudy of the Reformation. Justification by faith was called the "material principle" of the Reformation, and the doctrine of the Bible as the sole authority for faith and life was called the "formal principle." However, the Reformation had not separated these two. Justification was indeed held to be the central content of the Bible by the Reformers, but one could not understand the Bible as the norm for faith and life apart from the central idea of justification.[39] The two Reformation principles were interdependent. Here, as in many similar instances in theology, distinctions which are useful for the purposes of analysis should not be permitted to damage an original unity. As the Swedish professor Ragnar Bring says, if sanctification is separated from justification, "then we divide up into different elements what for the New Testament and Luther is a unity."[40]

Because theology is a living process, we have had occasion to observe many variations on the theme of justification from Luther up to the present century. We have taken a giant step if all we have learned is that particular theological insights never remain static, even when attempts are made to mold them into unchangeable shapes. Even when we affirm, with modern theology, that it is necessary to get behind traditional Lutheranism to recover Luther's own unique teachings on justification, we should not deceive ourselves that the past can give us a permanent statement about justification which will settle the issue for all time. That is precisely what Orthodoxy and Pietism attempted, but all their veneration of Luther could not prevent them from interpreting justification in the thought forms and according to the spiritual needs of their own day.

The task is not over, therefore, when we have recovered something of Luther's dynamic, personal understanding. As we shall see shortly, the questions preying on Luther's mind are not necessarily identical with the spiritual questions of our century.

> Theology has therefore an immensely difficult task: on the one hand, it must seek to go back to the world of the Bible and to Luther's theology, and discover there the way of thinking in which God's election, his predestination, his salvation, and his

justifying acts are clearly set forth, and thus safe-
guard what is of permanent worth in traditional
Christian doctrine, while, on the other hand, it
must so present this that men in our own time can
personally commit themselves to it.[41]

Justification Today

One can say without hesitation that the doctrine of
justification is enjoying a noticeable renewal. A dra-
matic symbol of this renaissance is the publication of
*Justification: The Doctrine of Karl Barth and a Catholic
Reflection* in 1957 (English translation, 1964).[42] The author of the book is a Swiss Catholic priest and theologian, Father Hans Küng, already well known for his
frank public criticisms of some of his church's practices, and recognized as an important theological ad-
viser in the work of the Second Vatican Council. Küng
argues that a comparison between the theology of
Karl Barth, famous contemporary Protestant theologian
of Basel, and the teaching, rightly understood, of the
sixteenth century Council of Trent (the Roman Catholic
council of 1545-63) reveals that there are substantial
areas of agreement on the very doctrine which for so
long has divided Roman Catholics and Protestants—
the doctrine of justification. The book includes a letter
from Barth to Küng in which the Protestant theologian
writes: "If what you have presented in Part Two of
this book is actually the teaching of the Roman Catholic Church, then I must certainly admit that my view
of justification agrees with the Roman Catholic view;
if only for the reason that the Roman Catholic teaching
would then be most strikingly in accord with mine!"[43]

Another symbol is the little book *Justification Today*
issued by the Lutheran World Federation's Commission
and Department of Theology in 1965. It reports dis-

cussions on justification before, during, and since the Fourth Assembly of the Lutheran World Federation which met in Helsinki, Finland, in 1963.[44] An American news magazine's article on that conference carried the subtitle "Justifying Justification." It reported the failure of the delegates to reach agreement on a modern statement of the classic Reformation doctrine. The news article also quoted Dr. Gerhard Gloege of Bonn University as saying, "It is an open secret that today neither the church nor the world knows what to do with this doctrine of justification. For the fathers it was the fountain and rule of faith and life. For the church today it is clearly an embarrassment."[45]

The lack of unanimity at Helsinki might be taken as the healthy willingness to make an honest reexamination of justification rather than embarrassment. The summary found in *Justification Today* ranges over several different approaches to the doctrine of justification —historical, confessional, biblical, practical. It is out of the question to cover in these observations the many suggestions and disagreements recorded. We shall content ourselves with a brief selection of ideas presented in the book with the prospect of returning to these and other points in our next chapter.

1. *Justification Today* frankly takes note of weaknesses in the Lutheran confessions, including the intellectual interpretation of faith in Article IV of the Augsburg Confession. The contributors are agreed that faith ought to be understood in a more personal way, the total commitment of the self to God in wholehearted trust. In other words, Lutherans today do not hesitate to draw upon Luther's dynamic view of faith in correcting later Lutheranism's tendency to see faith as knowledge of and assent to Christ's saving work.[46]

2. The contributors are willing to reexamine the

traditional Lutheran claim that justification is the central doctrine of Christianity, but they do not appear to have reached any clear-cut position on this point. Even those who wish to modify the Reformers' strong affirmation as to the centrality of justification do not deny the importance of this New Testament teaching. They suggest rather that justification, in the words of one proposal, "is a pure interpretation of the New Testament, but not the *only* pure interpretation."[47] Hence the Lutheran World Federation would recognize other churches as biblical even though they choose some other biblical language than justification.

3. An interesting point discussed was whether justification has to presuppose the terrified conscience which Luther experienced.[48] "Unlike Luther, Paul does not relate the doctrine of justification to the terrified conscience; Paul has a good conscience."[49] Some stressed the differences between Paul and Luther, between Luther and modern man. Others insisted that the differences are not to be overestimated; the burdened conscience is a common human problem of every age. If people today are not bothered by their sins, whether outward vices or sins of thought, the church must preach the law to convict man of his sin.[50]

4. In several different ways *Justification Today* shows the desire of the participants to speak of justification in a more comprehensive way. Traditionally, when Lutherans have stressed the forensic (or legal) aspect of justification they have done so to keep justification pure, sharply distinguished from all thoughts of works and merits. But there is much to be learned in relating justification to baptism, to eschatology, to the church, to the new life of the Christian, to Christ's victory over sin and death, and to man's vocation in the world.

5. On the whole, the book *Justification Today* discloses a willingness to discuss justification with the
needs of twentieth-century man in mind. One view is
that the questions of Paul or Luther are not the questions modern man is asking. Thus a restatement of
justification in more contemporary terms is needed.
Another view is that by preaching justification effectively the church will drive into the hearers' hearts the
question of their readiness to face the last judgment.
Especially apt is the observation that "the world of our
century is ruled by the basic principle of an exclusive
self-justification."[51]

Our selection of the five items above from *Justification Today* is arbitrary and in the interests of brevity
and convenience. The next chapter will provide occasions to refer to some of the thoughts expressed in this
valuable, up-to-date report on recent discussions of
justification.

How is justification presented by other modern
scholars? One conspicuous trend is to define justification with reference to the reestablishment of the right
relationship between God and man. That man apart
from Christ is a sinner who cannot save himself is a
teaching universally accepted. To cite a phrase from
a textbook used widely in colleges and seminaries, a
significant result of God's work in and through Jesus
Christ is "to restore men to a right relationship with
God in spite of their sins (justification)."[52] A recent
book on the theology of Paul makes a similar point in
speaking of righteousness. The author wants to avoid
the idea that justification confers a new status which
becomes a quality of the sinner. "It is safer, therefore,
to speak of justification not as a status or as a quality
but as a relationship."[53] As to righteousness, this is not
the sort of gift which the new owner now counts as his

own possession. "What God has gratuitously conferred upon men is a right relationship with Himself."[54]

Rudolf Bultmann is a controversial German New Testament scholar who might be expected to treat justification in a rather radical way. In some respects this is true, yet he can use the old Lutheran term "forensic" (or legal) with reference to Paul's idea of the righteousness of God. By this he means that a person does not have righteousness as something of his own but rather has it in the verdict of the "forum" (from whence we get the word "forensic").[55] It is an eschatological verdict (i.e., controlled by the future salvation) pronounced in the present. Righteousness is a present reality. But not an ethical quality. Therefore Bultmann writes, "When God rightwises the sinner, 'makes him righteous' (Rom. 4:5), that man is not merely 'regarded as if' he were righteous, but really is righteous—i.e. absolved from his sin by God's verdict."[56] So Bultmann too says that righteousness is not a quality of man but a relationship.[57] We have thus far met familiar Lutheran ideas in Bultmann: use of the term "forensic," placing forgiveness at the center of justification.

But when it comes to the meaning of faith, Bultmann will surprise many readers by declaring that faith is obedience. "Paul understands faith primarily as obedience; he understands the act of faith as an act of obedience."[58] At this point we understand why Bultmann is often described as an existentialist. The meaning of life is never found in abstractions, but in the immediacy of actual existence and decision. Faith as an act of obedience means that man gives up the understanding of himself which he formerly had and decides for the new self-understanding given him in the Gospel. Bultmann regards this existentialist approach as consistent with Lutheran teaching. The opposite of faith is works or, as he likes to say, "boasting."

In the act of obedience, which is faith, man gives up any righteousness of his own and obediently submits "to the God-determined way of salvation." Faith is not salvation itself; it is the condition for receiving salvation. It is interesting that Bultmann does not agree with Luther that faith is trust. Trust is included, but Bultmann associates trust with the consciousness of sin and repentance and these, he says, are somewhat rare expressions in Paul. We have noted, however, that in discussing the verdict of righteousness Bultmann does make explicit mention of being absolved from sin. But in the main, Bultmann would side with those who say that the apostle Paul had a good conscience. Considerations of repentance and forgiveness are less prominent than the obedience whereby man submits to God's pronouncement in the Gospel.[59]

The existentialist view of faith is to be preferred over that of a mental acceptance of doctrine. Bultmann wants to warn us against complacency in the Christian life. But there is a danger. It is true that man must exercise faith each time he is confronted with the Gospel, but it is also true that the believer is sustained in the ongoing life of faith. According to Bultmann, each moment seems to call for a fresh act of obedience starting, as it were, from the very beginning. In other words, the reality of the new birth is not considered. By faith man enters into the family of God where, by the continual working of the Spirit, the new life is given support through periods when faith is weak. Paul speaks frequently of being "in Christ." We exist as Christians in a new sphere, in the flock which the Good Shepherd tends. In short, one does not jump into and out of one's standing as a Christian as each moment confronts one with the decision of faith or unbelief. By accenting faith as obedient decision, Bultmann pictures the Christian's existence as a succession of separate moments instead of a continuing life of fellowship with Christ. His view is strong on decision but weak on continuity.

So far, these few soundings in the work of modern scholarship have demonstrated that justification involves a great many things. It is difficult to formulate a concise "definition" of justification which will cover all the aspects associated with this biblical term. It will also be made clear, as we turn to another scholar, that the topic of justification is of such complexity that one cannot readily classify theologians according to their respective views on justification.

Joachim Jeremias is a widely recognized German New Testament scholar, a Lutheran, who wants to tone down the suggestion of a forensic justification in order to make the point that "God's justification is an outpouring of grace which far exceeds the legal sphere."[60] On the other hand, Jeremias repeats a thought which is quite traditional among Lutherans when he writes, "Justification is forgiveness, nothing but forgiveness for Christ's sake."[61] At first glance this seems to narrow justification down too much, but Jeremias, with Luther, understands forgiveness in a comprehensive way. He cites Luther's well-known saying, "Where remission of sin is, there is life and salvation." Hence the remission of sin does not have only a negative function, that is, cancelling out the sinful past, but also a positive function, for which Jeremias coins the word "antedonation," meaning "a donation made in advance."[62] Justification bestows in the present time an anticipation of God's final gift. "As an antedonation of God's final acquittal, justification is pardon in the fullest sense. It is the beginning of a new life, a new existence, a new creation through the gift of the Holy Spirit."[63]

Jeremias, then, keeps justification clear of legal considerations; he interprets justification as forgiveness but that means the beginning of a new life. Next we note that Jeremias connects justification with baptism. Here too we may compare the contemporary German scholar with Luther, for both see baptism as extending its significance over one's whole life. Here are Luther's words in his *Treatise on Baptism:*

> This significance of baptism, viz., the dying or drowning of sin, is not fulfilled completely in this life, nay, not until man passes through bodily death also, and utterly decays to dust. . . . Therefore, so far as the sign of the sacrament and its significance are concerned, sins and the man are both already dead, and he has risen again, and so the sacrament has taken place; but the work of the sacrament has not yet been fully done, that is to say, death and the resurrection at the Last Day are yet before us.[64]

Modern theologians would say that Luther here presents an "eschatological" view of baptism, that is, a view which grasps that baptism is aiming toward the future, toward the "eschaton" (the last thing, literally). Eschatology is briefly defined as the doctrine of the last things, i.e. the teachings of the Bible regarding the end of history, the resurrection of the dead, the last judgment, and the final realization by the believer of the full blessings promised to faith. Baptism is "eschatological" because its significance, as Luther says, is not fulfilled completely in this life. Similarly, the other central teachings of the New Testament are eschatological in that they tell us about God's work in Christ which realizes its completion in the final culmination of all things. Does this include justification? Yes, most decidedly. Paul has a clear statement to this effect in Gal. 5:5: "For through the Spirit, by faith, we wait for the hope of righteousness." Jeremias explains this verse as follows: "Justification, then, is the beginning of a movement towards a goal, namely towards the hour of the definitive justification, of the acquittal on the day of judgment, when the full gift is realized."[65]

What is the advantage of connecting Paul's doctrine of justification with baptism? It enables Jeremias to give justification its due prominence without claiming that it is the only correct way of expressing Paul's basic understanding of the Gospel. The curious fact is that justification has been very prominent in Christian history, yet only three of Paul's epistles discuss "justification by faith" (Galatians, Romans, and Philippians). From this fact certain scholars of a previous generation drew the conclusion that justification was a secondary consideration for Paul.

But what they failed to do, according to Jeremias, was to ask, How is justification bestowed? The answer is, through baptism, with 1 Cor. 6:11 as a case in point: "But you were washed, you were sanctified, you were justified in the name of the Lord Jesus Christ and in the Spirit of our God." Here the verb "to be justified" is "surrounded by baptismal terms and formulae."[66] The main argument for connecting justification and baptism is that Paul as an active missionary knew that it was in baptism that the benefits of Christ's work were bestowed. The connection was so obvious for him that it was not necessary at every point to put into words that justification by faith is implied in baptism and that baptism is the act whereby those who believe in Jesus Christ are included in the fellowship of Christians.

Furthermore, baptismal language was probably more familiar to people than the language of justification.

A Look Back and a Look Ahead

Justification involves both God and man. The first chapter in this book tried to understand, without scolding and preaching, that all men are interested in being justified, whether they are conscious of theological implications or not. The second chapter describes the work of God in Christ for the justification of men. Paul's main emphasis seemed to be, as Jeremias rightly observes, on Christ's death and resurrection as the basis for man's justification. To get at how things look from man's side, one has to draw inferences from what Paul and other New Testament writers have to say. The survey of what churchmen have said about justification in the present chapter revealed efforts to understand what justification accomplishes in the sphere of human experience. At the same time, we have noted the insistence that justification is not man's doing but the work of God.

You and I come upon the scene in the next chapter. What does it mean *for us* that God in Christ justifies those who believe? What is it like to be justified? In answering these questions we want to come as close as we can to our own situation in life. But in doing so we will find that justification continues to be, as Paul taught, the activity of God. The wonder of all this is that the more we learn about the working of God in our own lives, the more we learn about God himself.

4.

If God Be for Us

The title of this chapter and of the book is taken from Rom. 8:31. In its context, the phrase looks like this:

> What then shall we say to this? If God is for us, who is against us? He who did not spare his own Son but gave him up for us all, will he not also give us all things with him? Who shall bring any charge against God's elect? It is God who justifies (Rom. 8:31-33).

What do we experience when we are justified by faith? A beginning answer lies in this passage, taken from the Revised Standard Version of the Bible. The chapter title itself is from the King James translation which uses the word "be" where RSV chooses "is." The Greek text does not help us decide between the two readings because it has no verb whatever! To paraphrase Luther, we are interested here in speaking English, not Greek. The sense and tone of the King James phrase, "If God be for us," seems to us to be more robust and emphatic than the RSV's milder "If God is for us." In both cases the "if" does not mean something uncertain and questionable. Rather, it means "since" and the same is true in Rom. 6:8, "But if [or since] we have died with Christ, we believe that we shall also live with him." In the sixth chapter of Romans Paul has already affirmed that the believers *have* died with Christ in baptism (Rom. 6:3-4), therefore the "if" in the later verse actually affirms a fact. So it is in Rom. 8:31: God being for us is a fact to be affirmed. Since God is for us, there isn't anyone against us whose opposition needs to be feared.

The next verse, Rom. 8:32, achieves two things. First, it marks God's giving of his own Son on the cross as evidence that God is indeed for us. But more than that, the gift of the Son is accompanied with a promise of further gifts in the present and the future. "Will he not also give us all things with him?"

Rom. 8:33 in the King James Version says vividly, "Who shall lay anything to the charge of God's elect?" The key verb here is a legal term. The image is that of a court of law where someone is accused. Our English translations tone down the force of the thought Paul is expressing here. Another way to translate would be: "Who is going to bring an accusation against the elect of God? God himself?!! God, the One who justifies?" This paraphrase might be criticized for introducing a question mark in order to dramatize the incredibility of God's being thought of as the one who accuses his own. But even without the device of using a question mark we can bring out the same vigorous insistence by Paul that it is impossible to place God in the role of accuser. "Who is going to bring an accusation against the elect of God? God is the very one who justifies!!"

We find in Luther a similar combined paraphrase and commentary on this same passage. He writes: "Who shall lay anything to the charge of God's elect? Nobody. Why? Because it is God who justifies. Who is it that shall condemn? Nobody. Why? It is Jesus Christ (who is very God) who died, nay rather, who is risen again. If God be for us, then, who can be against us?"[1]

Now what practical, personal, and contemporary significance does justification have for us whose task is to worship and serve God in the twentieth century? The answer must be based on the biblical conviction that God is indeed for us because of Jesus Christ. *That God is for us expresses the essential meaning of justification.* You are on the freeway driving home after a demanding day at work. It is hot and the traffic is heavy. You don't feel at all religious at the moment. But at that moment and right there, in your not-yet-paid-for car, God is for you! He is in your behalf. He claims you and you are his. It is fine if you manage to reflect on this fact as you wait for the traffic light to change. But the fact is on record whether you think about justification or not. God happens to care very much for people driving along on freeways. If justification can't be true then, when will a better time arrive?

There is nothing to wait for before entering into the experience of justification. When Jesus called disciples, they got up and followed him. They didn't wait for him to supply them with full explanations of who he was and what they were to do. The Gospel calls for an immediate act of faith. Justification is part of that Gospel. It says, in all simplicity, "God is to be trusted. Trust him and be justified."

Christ and Justification

In the New Testament, Christ is the key to and content of justification. What does that mean? That Christ makes justification possible? Indeed. That the forgiveness of sins, which is always implied in justification, was made possible by Christ's life, death, and resurrection? Most emphatically, yes. That Christ and only Christ furnishes the power by which the Christian embarks on a new life of sonship and service? Yes, indeed. And such statements could be multiplied.

It is when statements lead us to experience that language is doing its job. At this point in our study we are especially attentive to justification as something we experience in very concrete terms. When we make the statement, "Christ is the key to and content of justification," we are referring to a reality which invades our actual existence. How does this happen?

Rom. 3:22, discussed in detail in the second chapter, provides the answer in the words, "the righteousness of God *through [the] faithfulness of Jesus Christ* for all who believe." Remember the bridge. The faithfulness of Jesus was the bridge connecting the righteousness of God on one side with the response of man on the other. We tried to make clear that the righteousness of God is not an abstract quality, but God's active disposition to save men. The faithfulness of Jesus Christ is the historical form taken by that active disposition on God's part. God does not content himself with the issuing of statements about himself and his intentions. He moves into action in human history, and the whole life of Jesus is that saving action.

Maybe we should revise the children's favorite Sunday school song, "Jesus loves me, this I know, for the Bible tells me so." Rightly understood, the Bible tells me so by placing before my eyes the living Christ. Excusing the meter, try this on your piano: "God is righteous this I know, Jesus' faithfulness tells me so." We have found this to be a basic Pauline clue to the meaning of justification. Both in Rom. 3:22 and in Gal. 2:16 the sequence of ideas is the same: God's action in the faithfulness of Christ leads to man's faith and justification. But again, this arrangement of ideas really

describes events that are happening. To underscore
this process of events, we have to reflect for a moment
on two stages of the work of Christ.

The first stage is Christ's historical work, from Beth-
lehem to the resurrection. Throughout his earthly life,
Jesus displayed faithfulness to God in all things. The
fact of his faithfulness provides history with tangible
data that God is a just and loving God. But how are
people to believe that this is so? Not merely by being
told on church authority that this is good theology.
There is a much better way. And that is to open up
the Gospel records by Matthew, Mark, Luke, and John.
The narratives contained in the four Gospels all have
the same purpose of allowing us to witness the actions
of the living Lord. We hear Jesus telling parables; we
see him perform miracles; we observe him in contro-
versy; we see him healing the sick and casting out
demons; we trace his steps to Jerusalem and the cross;
finally there are reports, confused and uncertain at
first, that something unexpected has taken place. Jesus'
body is no longer in the tomb, they say; he is risen from
the dead!

The entire drama is saying that God is overcoming
the skepticism of mankind regarding the possibility
that there ever could be any genuine righteousness
here on earth. God's own righteousness is on display in
Jesus' faithful life. Jesus is faithful to God, and God
proves his faithfulness not only to Jesus but to mankind
as a whole when he raises Jesus from the dead. All of
this is the ground of our justification. When we say
that Christ is the content of justification, we cannot be
content with a mere reference to his identity. Many
people do this, thinking that the point of the Gospels
is to tell us that Jesus is the Son of God. Others go a
little farther, mentioning that Jesus died on the cross

for us. These are, of course, correct observations, but they bypass the essential stuff and significance of Jesus' life in favor of easily-memorized doctrinal statements.

The second stage of Christ's work is going on today. We may call it the ministry of the risen Christ. Here too we have to struggle against ingrained habits of thought which deprive us of the full impact of divine reality. The content of our justification is Christ in his historical work and in his activity as the risen Lord. Because Christ appeared at a certain time in history, it is natural for the Christian to look back. However, the backward look is not enough for faith and justification. Our lives have to be given content today, in the present. The history of Jesus the Christ began in the first century, but it continues in the present. Our evidence for this is the resurrection and exaltation of Jesus. In short, the risen Christ is the content of our day-by-day experience of justification.

If we hold that the Christian life implies the constant exercise of faith, it is just as true that there is a constant experience of being justified. Paul writes in Rom. 5:1, "Therefore, since we are justified by faith, we have peace with God through our Lord Jesus Christ." The verbs are clearly in the present tense. When we grasp that justification continues to take place in daily life, we are liberated from the feeling that the Christian life is a heavy burden which we are required to bear alone. Instead, we hear the Gospel of the resurrection in a new way. The risen Christ is with us. God continues to honor the faithfulness of his Son so that at any moment I can be confident that God judges my own existence as a positive, worthwhile reality.

Some groups within Protestantism have so sharply accentuated justification as a decisive experience at the beginning of the Christian life that they picture the subsequent walk of the Christian man as something he does in his own strength. Such a view has a noble motive: it makes the distinction between justification and sanctification (or growth) very clear. However, it often results in the idea that justification belongs to the past; it is over and done with. Now man is on his own, living under that heavy burden of trying to become more sanctified.

Against such thinking we maintain that justification accompanies faith throughout our earthly lives. It is still entirely the work of God. There is no thought of man now contributing some portion, however small, of his salvation. The insistence on faith does not permit the reentry of works as a means toward justification. Faith constantly lays hold on Christ; God constantly justifies us through the faithfulness of Jesus Christ. Let us look at this from another perspective.

Justification is the work of the living God. He works in a particular way, through the earthly and risen life of Jesus Christ, his faithful Son. That work continues in history as God reaches into our lives. How? Through Christ. Yes, and who is Christ? We may answer in good traditional language: true God and true man. Did you hear correctly? Did someone say "true man"? Jesus was—and *is*—true man. Far from being a novel teaching, or a remnant of "liberalism," this is one of the ancient church's first and most important claims about Jesus. Jesus' humanity is at the heart of our justification; it has been implied all along in our repeated references to his faithfulness.

In justification we have God on our side, upholding us as men, confirming us in our humanity. What is it to be a man, to be human? The only answer is to look to Jesus Christ, the true man. On the whole, western Christendom has not been too much interested in the idea of man's becoming divine. It has stressed the difference between God and man. A side result of this emphasis has been to overlook, to our loss, the humanity of Jesus and with it the humanizing power of Jesus Christ. God does not invite us to become gods; rather, he places before us in Christ the possibility of realizing our true manhood. But there is more to say.

Justification and the Meaning of My Life

Notice that our topic does not promise that "the meaning of life" can be discovered through the doctrine of justification. We shall be more modest and more personal: the meaning of *my* life. If you and I find some meaning in our own lives, we may perhaps gather some inkling of the perennial question which we usually associate with the philosopher's domain, What is the meaning of life? But that is not our aim in this discussion. Having said that Christ is the content of our justification, we continue to press for the practical significance of "being justified" in our own existence.

The question of the meaning of one's personal existence has become in our day a very popular issue. This is due to the writings of existentialists (whether novelists, philosophers, poets, or theologians) and to the display of their reflections in various public media such as books, plays, and movies. Closely related to the quest for meaning has been the hunger for personal identity in a world where impersonal forces seem to make man isolated and lonely. "Who am I?" is a question being asked with great earnestness, not just by self-styled eccentrics but by very serious-minded people, both young and old.

Oddly enough, church people are often hesitant to reflect on the meaning of their lives, although they

ought to be among those most concerned. Perhaps
one reason for this is the fairly common notion that
the pastor should look into such things and tell us from
the pulpit what the meaning of our existence is supposed to be. What little reflective thinking is done by
the layman continues to be colored by a moralistic
outlook. "I know I am not what I should be," is a typical comment, spoken with apologetic resignation. Despite years and years of exposure to the Gospel of
justification by grace through faith, many Christians
still face life with a basically grim attitude, nursing the
forlorn hope that with a little more effort, a greater
degree of commitment and a purer attitude of sincerity,
they might someday reach the point where they can
come to terms with themselves.

Yet these good folks know a good many of the les-
sons of the Bible, including the one which says that we
are not justified by works of the law. It has not occurred
to them that "works of the law" are not confined to
ancient Pharisaic efforts; many of those nagging, inner
accusations are related to more modern forms of justification by works. It is even possible that the great news
of justification through Christ can be "heard" in such
a way that some will translate it into law. "Christ has
done his part," some will say, "now it's up to us." And
at that everyone in the vicinity looks very solemn, very
unworthy, very religious. Heads nod slowly in reverent
agreement. Someone else is seized by the spirit of this
solemn, defeatist, man-centered theology and offers
the opinion, "Yes, everything depends on us as indi-
viduals." Perhaps a quotation from a recent sermon will
clinch this point.

What is going on here? God and Christ and the work
of redemption are all being put out of sight back in
the distant past. God's part is over; now man is in

charge. Such scenes are discouraging, but their real-
ism increases our zeal to set forth the biblical teaching
of justification. Christ as the content of justification
means that God is still the chief actor in our lives. It is
not true that "everything depends on us." If we believe
in Christ, he is among us and in us. As of this moment,
the living Christ vouches for my personal existence and
gives it meaning. I am identified with Christ and his
company through baptism in his name. "I have been
crucified with Christ; it is no longer I who live, but
Christ who lives in me; and the life I now live in the
flesh I live by faith in the Son of God, who loved me
and gave himself for me" (Gal. 2:20). In light of what
we said a little earlier about modern forms of justification by works, we add a thought from the next verse
where Paul writes, "If justification were through the
law, then Christ died to no purpose" (Gal. 2:21).

The modern churchman needs help in recognizing
that society's standards of success have the effect of
pushing him toward a self-acceptance based on accom-
plishments. The drive to do well need not be in the
interests of a vulgar materialism. These compulsive efforts to succeed may carry such respectable labels as
"being a good provider," "meeting my responsibilities," or "being a credit to my profession." Moreover,
we said in the first chapter that man's desire to justify
himself belongs to the pattern of any society which
values order and communal responsibility. But the
Gospel of justification does not stop with general
human values; it points the way to an interpretation of
personal existence which frees man from the pressure
to achieve while at the same time it places his responsibilities in a new perspective.

For the apostle Paul, justification was the answer
to the problem of how Jewish and Gentile Christians

could realize their oneness in Christ; for Luther, justification was the answer to the problem of finding a gracious God. For you and me and our friends in this century, justification can provide the answer to still another question: How can I be assured that there is genuine worth, validity, and meaning in who I am and in what I do with my life? Disappointment and discouragement are sure to come if we accept as final the world's "law of achievement." But release, joy, and new appetite for living result when we believe the Gospel of justification. For that Gospel message—though it speaks of many other benefits for the person who is justified by faith—surely declares an end to the need to justify oneself. Even more amazing is the declaration that God himself in Christ gives validity to our lives.

A good way to appreciate this freedom from self-justification and freedom for affirming life on God's terms is to consider Luther's doctrine of vocation. If justification is to mean anything at all, it must reach me where I live and work. But if it is just a Sunday doctrine, part of the mental furniture that goes with the visible church furniture, it will remain imprisoned within a special set of "religious" associations. But the Gospel never intends that theology be kept separate from daily life. Luther encourages us to glory in our calling, our vocation, and within that vocation realize the full possibilities of being free children of God.

Take the case of a high school student. The "law of achievement" which permeates our culture tells the high school youth that he will be justified in the future, for then he will accomplish something for which he will be recognized. For the present time he is "only a student." The best he can hope for is a good record which will qualify him for entrance to a good college which in turn will prepare him for a well-paying job, and eventually society will take notice that he has made the grade. But the Gospel, as God's power for salvation to every one who has faith, sets the student free as one who is *now* justified in the sight of God and, we must be sure to add, in the sight of the community of believers.

Now, right now, our high school friend is one whose life has validity. And not just because he serves as an acolyte on Sunday morning. Not because he is one of the officers in the church's youth group. It is not *as youth leader* or *as choir member* or *as acolyte* that he is justified. It is *as young man or young lady* whose calling is that of *high school student*. God justifies the specific existence of this young person. God bestows meaning and worth upon this young life here and now in his calling *as high school student*.

Each of us can adapt the illustration to himself. The temptation is to conclude from the message of justification that God justifies us in our role as faithful church members or with respect to special spiritual problems. The glory of justification is that God justifies us as insurance salesmen, as housewives, as business executives, as department store clerks, as delivery boys, as high school principals, as astronauts, as custodians— as whatever we are and do in the normal pursuits of daily existence. But let us be careful lest we empty the glory of justification by tacking on a condition to the effect that God justifies the outstanding performers only. That would lead us straight back to the "law of achievement" from which we have been delivered.

One doesn't need to know much psychology to realize that dissatisfaction with oneself is a common source of personal unhappiness. The hardest misfortunes to bear are those in which we are convinced that we have failed. The basketball player who fails to make the crucial free throw finds it hard to live with himself for a few days. The housewife whose dessert turns out to be a mess is not consoled when the guests praise the tenderness of the roast. The conscientious parent is more disturbed by his own loss of self-control in berating the children than by the minor mischief they have been up to. All of these disruptions, trivial as they are, have a way of causing us to ask just what sort of persons we are. The anguish within is really a longing for justification, an unuttered cry for someone to assure us that we still count, that our foolishness has not destroyed our validity as persons, our right to be! Faith, which is never easy, is equal to such moments because God in Christ justifies the ungodly. We need not look for the basis of justification in ourselves or our performance because it lies outside of ourselves, in Jesus Christ and his faithfulness.

Therefore the claim that Christ is the content of justification is not just conventional religious language. It means that my own life is in vital connection with the greatest life ever lived. By faith I share in everything Jesus was and did. Orthodox theologians of past centuries have said that God *imputes* (transfers) the righteousness of Christ to the believing sinner. The trouble with this approach is that Christ is pictured as one whose moral perfection before the law is transferred to us. The imputation of righteousness seen in this way means that it is the law, after all, which is the sovereign norm for all of mankind. Even when we are justified through Christ, the ultimate significance of justification is that we are squared with the law.

There is greater power in the Gospel than that! The work of Jesus Christ does not reach its high point in the satisfaction of the demands of the law. It culminates, rather, in the victory of Christ over sin, death, and all evil powers, and the victory is shared by the followers of Christ. As Paul writes in Rom. 8:32, "He who did not spare his own Son but gave him up for us all, will he not also give us all things with him?" The powers of the resurrection, the powers of the new age, the creative powers of new life are offered to those who are justified by faith in Christ. It is on this side of the resurrection that Christ becomes the content of our justification. As the Swedish theologian Ragnar Bring writes in commenting on justification in Galatians, "But men were taken up into this work of God, for justification meant incorporation in Christ; men died and rose again with him."[2]

Bring's reference to incorporation in Christ deserves a further comment, for it bears on the question of how God's work in Christ is to be related to man's appropriation of divine action. Orthodoxy seemed to rely largely on the mind's acceptance of the fact that God had made a favorable declaration. Pietism wanted to understand justification as warm-hearted experience. The Age of Rationalism could only link justification with moral improvement, and the nineteenth century had room for variants of all these views. Some immediately conclude that the twentieth century's contribution to the question of how the grace of God in Christ is brought home to man is religious existentialism. Although the Danish philosopher Kierkegaard lived in the last century, it is the present century which has given serious heed to his characterization of faith as a leap, or as we often say, a total commitment. The German New Testament scholar referred to earlier, Rudolf Bultmann, reflects something of this Kierkegaardian idea when he describes faith as radical obedience.

A less heralded but significant way of grasping how

the saving work of Christ and the man of faith come together is suggested in Bring's statement noted above, namely, "incorporation in Christ." Many New Testament scholars of this century have caught sight of this important feature of Paul's thought. Paul can state it in a very disarming way simply by saying that those who believe in Christ are "in Christ" (e.g., "if any one is in Christ, he is a new creation" 2 Cor. 5:17). To be "in Christ" is to be incorporated in him. Christ and those who believe in him constitute one corporate entity. As Paul writes in Gal. 3:26-27: "for in Christ Jesus you are all sons of God, through faith. For as many of you as were baptized into Christ have put on Christ."

We have been inquiring into the topic of justification and the meaning of my life. It is Christ who supplies a meaning to my existence because when I am justified through faith in him I am freed from the necessity of making my life valid by means of achievements. Positively, the meaning of my life is given in and through my specific vocation, not in special, self-conscious religious pursuits. These are splendid things to claim! There is a firm basis for claiming them in the fact of our incorporation into Christ in faith and baptism.

The liberal theology of the early part of this century held up Jesus as an example which we should follow. The so-called neo-orthodoxy of the forties and fifties was more appreciative of Christ's passion and resurrection, calling for faith as the reestablishment of the right relationship between God and man. Throughout recent decades we have also been rediscovering that the Christian is not an isolated atom floating about the universe, finding God only in the secrecy of private meditation; the Christian belongs to the community of Christians, to the body of Christ. He is made a member of this body by baptism, he is sustained in the fellowship by participation in the Lord's Supper, he confesses his faith in Christ in concert with other believers, and he shares with them the certain hope of the final victory of Christ, the Lord of the universe.

What does this suggest as to the meaning of my life? It suggests a dimension of justification that is waiting to be claimed and enjoyed, namely, the dimension of corporate Christian experience. In justification I meet my brother because Christ has ruled out works and achievements as the basis on which we come together. In the fellowship of the church there is a welcome for the nonachievers, the inferiority complexes, the timid, the no-talented. But that is not all. These same people —and we are among them—*receive* something in the fellowship. They receive dignity, worth, standing, validity. It will even happen that once liberated from the depressing law of achievement, we discover that by God's grace we *can* do something, we *can* contribute to the building up of the body. And this same phenomenon of discovering one's worth in the midst of God's people carries over into our lives as citizens and neighbors. The justified man, no longer frantic about earning acceptance, is now gloriously free to serve his neighbor and his world. Justification has delivered him from blustering self-assertion and cringing self-pity. As Luther says, in faith he has everything, so he is free to love. And in the practice of love he discovers—without looking for it—the meaning of his life.

God Is Righteous

We are nearing the end of our study in the meaning of justification. When it is impossible to say everything that could be said on such a profound subject, one

tries to say the most important things. In this chapter
we are hoping to touch on the most important implications of justification in the three subtopics: Christ
and justification; justification and the meaning of my
life; God is righteous.

While it has not always been said in so many words,
I have hoped to contend in this little book that justification is justification and not something else. Much
as I appreciate the inescapable fact that justification
can be related to just about everything else in the New
Testament, I do not think that it serves the purpose to
argue, for example, that justification is forgiveness. Or
that justification is the same as reconciliation. Or that
it is simply another way of saying that we are saved.
Of course, the justified man receives the forgiveness
of sins, is reconciled to God, and is saved. But I am
convinced, out of respect for Paul's own vocabulary,
that justification has its own intrinsic message to report.
And in line with that conviction I have tried to keep
the idea of God's righteousness close at hand. "Righteousness" and "justification" are not only derived
from the same root word; they bear a necessary theological relationship to one another.

This thought is fortified by Rom. 3:26: "it was to
prove at the present time that he [God] himself is
righteous and that he justifies him who has faith in
Jesus." Justification can be meaningful theologically
only when a *just* or *righteous* God does the justifying.
Justification is meaningful in practical and personal
terms when the realization finally seeps through the
believer's consciousness that the most objective judgment conceivable in the whole universe, that of God
himself, has been passed on his life, and that God's
unequivocal declaration is that this man's life is worth
while!

At this point our theological indoctrination quickly raises a qualification. "Ah, but it is only a declaration. We are regarded *as if* we were righteous, *as if* we had never sinned. It isn't *really* so." True, it isn't really so that we have never sinned, but what about the other "as if"? We agree with Bultmann that this insistence on "as if" in the case of our being righteous rests upon the misunderstanding of regarding righteousness as an ethical quality. Reformation theology has correctly kept the problem of sin clearly in view, not only in the case of the unregenerate man but also in the case of the child of God who is justified and sinning at the same time.

It is good to have this constant reminder before us. But we have the right and the solemn duty to take God at his word. Another New Testament scholar whom we have cited before, Professor Jeremias, writes in this connection: "God's acquittal is not only forensic, it is not an 'as if,' not a mere word, but it is God's word that works and creates life. God's word is always an effective word."[3] When God in Jesus Christ "reckons righteousness" to the believers (Rom. 4:3-13), then we are not free to decide that here is something other than righteousness. Similarly, when we are told in 2 Cor. 5:21, "For our sake he made him to be sin who knew no sin, so that in him we might become the righteousness of God," it is not fitting to empty the term "righteousness" of all but some fictional meaning.

We always want to remain on the alert against human self-righteousness. We are glad to recognize, with our forefathers, that God is the source and giver of all righteousness. Nevertheless, the "righteousness of faith" (Rom. 4:13) must be taken seriously. It is gratifying to observe how Professor Ragnar Bring expresses this thought with uncluttered directness in his article on Justification in *The Encyclopedia of the Lutheran Church*. He speaks at one point " . . . of the biblical and theological meaning of justification, the divine act of making sinful men righteous."[4] At a later point in the article he gives us this fuller statement: "Again, justification can only be understood rightly as an expression for the Bible's view of the action of the righteous God by which he gives man a share in his righteousness. In God's action righteousness and love are one."[5]

Something curious has taken place in Protestant thought about justification over the years. There was a powerful motivation in Luther and his successors to rule out human achievement and to give all glory to God. To make sure that justification by grace through faith would continue to underscore the initiative and sovereign power of God, it was deemed wise and necessary to make constant reference to the sinful condition of man. The intended effect of these repeated reminders concerning man's sin and guilt was to make clear that man could not save himself—that he was utterly dependent upon God's grace in Christ.

But the lesson was learned too well, as it were. Since man's sinfulness now stood out as the all-consuming problem to be faced, justification came to be interpreted more and more as the solution to this problem. Hence, as we have noted several times, justification was interpreted as essentially identical with the forgiveness of sins. Moreover, preoccupation with man's sinfulness made justification take on more and more of a man-centered coloring. In other words, you talk about justification when you talk about man. It has to do with man and his needs.

In the meantime, what of the righteousness of God? The answer to that was easily supplied. God is and remains righteous. Man, of course, is unrighteous. The function of God's righteousness becomes a psychological one. That is, it is a good thing to mention it once in a while—along with God's holiness—just to show the contrast between God and man. Whenever man threatens to become too arrogant, he can be shamed into remorse by extolling the awesome righteousness of God. In the Lutheran family, this is not at all an exaggerated version of what is called "preaching the law." References to the righteousness of God, according to this thinking, are useful tools in driving home the contrast between God and man, thus making clear man's sinful, lost condition. Notice that this reasoning takes for granted that the term which serves as the natural partner for God's righteousness is the term "law." We recall, however, that according to Pauline teaching it is in the Gospel that the righteousness of God is revealed (Rom. 1:16-17). But the main point is that justification has bit by bit lost its proper God-centered character and has become man-centered. We no longer talk about the righteousness of God except when it is necessary to scare the unrepentant. If we do occasionally speak of man as being reckoned righteous through faith, the emphasis is on *reckoned,* not on *righteous.* "It isn't *really* so."

But it is. God is righteous, and he brings about righteousness on earth among and through men whom he justifies. When someone is justified by faith, declared righteous, then there is righteousness. According to Paul, the historic revelation of the righteousness of God was "through the faithfulness of Jesus Christ" (Rom. 3:22). The faithfulness of Jesus Christ continues as an operative power in history through his risen life, through the Gospel, and through the "lives of all faithful and godly men." Rom. 3:24-25 is a passage packed full of great biblical terms describing the significance of Christ's work: justified, redemption, expiation. And why all this? Paul's answer is clear: "This was to show God's righteousness." And he adds in the next sentence, "it was to prove at the present time that he himself is righteous and that he justifies him who has faith in Jesus" (Rom. 3:26).

Someone has said that this latter sentence is one of the boldest statements in the entire Bible. God actually goes out of his way to demonstrate his own righteousness! He wants to show mankind that his action in Jesus Christ is the right thing to do. So we come back to a thought expressed much earlier in this book: when Paul deals with the problem of righteousness in Romans, chapter 3, he makes clear that it is *God's* righteousness that really matters. Luther long ago noticed the same thing. His words of comment startle and perhaps dismay us when we first look at them: "For that passive Justification of God with which he is justified by us is itself our active justification by God. For he counts as justice, that faith which regards his words as just, for 'the just lives by faith.'. . ."[6]

What are we to make of such strange words? Is Luther actually saying that a kind of two-way process is going on in justification? Yes, God's action and man's response are intimately related. In another place Luther writes that God "is justified in his words, i.e. when he is believed in the gospel concerning the fulfillment of his promise."[7] Once we have learned from Paul that God proves that he is righteous, it is not so difficult to follow Luther's comments. We justify God by believing his promises; God justifies us when we believe, when we take him to be trustworthy.[8] Faith is counted as justice, which is really only a restatement of Rom. 4:5, "his faith is reckoned as righteousness." The fundamental point here is that God's righteousness is not a static quality used only to inspire fear but rather an activity which brings about, through Christ and through faith, justice or righteousness here on earth among men.

In the previous section we discussed justification in relation to our finding meaning in our lives. Simply put, the point was that in Christ God places worth and value upon our lives, freeing us from self-justification and incorporating us into Christ. Glorious as it is to receive this new lease on life when we discover that God places his endorsement on our existence, it does not exhaust the full meaning of being justified by faith. In fact, there might be a danger that a one-sided emphasis on God's justification of my life "just as I am" could lead to ethical indifference and a lack of appreciation of what God's long-range plan is when he so justifies me. We might very easily lapse back into the very passivity and quietism which is frequently the occasion of severe criticism on the part of those who hold that the Reformation was weak with respect to setting man on his feet to face up to his responsibilities. Another way of putting it is to say that if it is a mistake to interpret justification solely as the forgiveness of sins, it is a similar mistake to interpret justification solely as an invitation to bask in God's gracious bestowal of meaning upon my life. In either case, we would be guilty of reducing the Gospel to a private benefit to be enjoyed far away from the world's strife.

Therefore we are concluding our study by returning to the starting point: the righteousness of God. The very fact that this term reminds us of the Old Testament, of Israel and the prophets, provides a wider perspective for our final thought on justification. As we know, the New Testament story about Jesus is the climax of a long history of God's involvement in the life of his people. One could sum up that story by saying that God has been at work for centuries to establish righteousness here on earth. The great prophets of Israel and Judah had special perception in discerning God's quest for righteousness. Lesser minds seem to have a fatal disposition to understand righteousness on their own terms instead of on God's terms. Righteousness is not merely good behavior, though it always involves the call to the highest levels of conduct. The prophets and Jesus and Paul saw that righteousness is primarily the working out in history of God's essential character of righteousness and love.

As we have seen, the New Testament declares that God's righteousness is revealed in the Gospel and shared with believing men. It follows, then, that what we earlier referred to as "God's long-range plan" is carried forward in the lives of believing men and women. Here we have in mind the church and its mission, the redemptive purpose of God for the world, the influence of the Gospel in the affairs of men. Many such familiar expressions are available to us when we wish to speak of God as living and active in this world, moving toward the goal of bringing the whole universe to an acknowledgment of Jesus as Lord (Phil. 2:10-11). One of the great Servant Songs in Isaiah gives a foretaste of the universal scope of God's justifying activity: "By his knowledge shall the righteous one, my servant, make many to be accounted righteous" (Isa. 53:11).

We suggest, then, that not until we have taken into account the whole purpose of God have we finished with the implications of the biblical doctrine of justification. We have learned that justification is to be understood eschatologically—meaning that as far as believers are concerned, "we wait for the hope of righteousness" (Gal. 5:5). There is also a sense in which the whole universe is awaiting the culmination of God's work. But the justified man does not merely wait in a passive manner; he places himself at God's disposal (cf. Rom. 12:1). As God's man in this world, he allies himself with God's age-old drive toward justice. In this alliance he knows the companionship of the suffering and risen Son of God.

To be justified by faith is to have one's life validated by God. That is a privilege beyond compare. But a deeper dimension is offered to every justified sinner: he is made a vital part of God's redeeming purpose in the world.

Footnotes

CHAPTER I

1. Joseph Stump, *An Explanation of Luther's Small Catechism,* Revised Edition (Philadelphia: Fortress Press, 1935) p. 91.

CHAPTER II

1. Gerhard Kittel (ed.), *Theological Dictionary of the New Testament,* trans. and ed. G. W. Bromiley (Grand Rapids: Eerdmans Publishing Co., 1964), II, 224. Used by permission.
2. *Ibid.,* II, 223.
3. *Ibid.,* II, 221.
4. *Ibid.*
5. *Ibid.,* II, 221-222.
6. Nils A. Dahl, "The Social Setting of the Doctrine of Justification," *Reflection,* Vol. 63 (March, 1966), p. 3.
7. J. C. Hoekendijk, *The Church Inside Out* (Philadelphia: The Westminster Press, 1966), p. 21.
8. An esteemed teacher, Dr. Otto A. Piper, first made me aware of what this translation implies. Cf. also Karl Barth's translation: "even the righteousness of God through his faithfulness in Jesus Christ unto all them that believe." Karl Barth, *The Epistle to the Romans,* trans. from sixth edition by Edwyn C. Hoskyns (London: Oxford University Press, 1933), p. 91.
9. See above, pp. 32-34.
10. N. H. Snaith, "Grace," *A Theological Word Book of the Bible,* ed. Alan Richardson (London: SCM Press, 1950), p. 101. Published in the United States by The Macmillan Company.
11. J. S. Whale, *Christian Doctrine* (Cambridge: University Press, 1956), p. 84.
12. C. K. Barrett, *The Epistle to the Romans* (New York: Harper & Row, London: A. & C. Black Ltd., 1957), pp. 79-80.
13. *Ibid.,* p. 79.

CHAPTER III

1. Gordon Rupp, *The Righteousness of God:* Luther Studies (London: Hodder and Stoughton, 1953), p. 145.
2. See 2 Corinthians 5:21. Roland H. Bainton, *Here I Stand: A Life of Martin Luther* (New York, Nashville: Abingdon Press, 1950), p. 62.

118   *If God Be for Us*

3. John Dillenberger and Claude Welch, *Protestant Christianity Interpreted Through Its Development* (New York: Charles Scribner's Sons, 1954), p. 19.
4. See Bainton, *Here I Stand,* p. 65.
5. Gordon Rupp, *The Righteousness of God,* pp. 121-122. Rupp refers to the Weimar edition of Luther's works, *W.A.,* 54. 179-87.
6. Heinrich Boehmer, *Road to Reformation:* Martin Luther to the Year 1521 (Philadelphia: Fortress Press, 1946), p. 110.
7. Rupp, *op. cit.,* pp. 180-181.
8. See Warren A. Quanbeck, "Luther's Early Exegesis," in *Luther Today* (Decorah, Iowa: Luther College Press, 1957), pp. 62-81.
9. *Ibid.,* p. 67.
10. Cited by Rupp, *The Righteousness of God,* p. 170. W.A. 56 298.22.
11. Cited by Rupp, *op. cit.,* p. 171. W.A. 56. 204.14.
12. J. S. Whale, *The Protestant Tradition* (Cambridge: University Press, 1955), p. 70.
13. Martin Luther, "A Treatise on Good Works," *Works of Martin Luther,* The Philadelphia Edition (Philadelphia: Fortress Press, 1943), I, 194.
14. Cf. T. A. Kantonen, *Resurgence of the Gospel* (Philadelphia: Fortress Press, 1948), p. 67.
15. Joseph Stump, *An Explanation of Luther's Small Catechism,* Revised Edition (Philadelphia: Fortress Press, 1935), p. 46.
16. *Works of Martin Luther,* I, 194-195.
17. *Ibid.,* I, 103-104.
18. *Works of Martin Luther,* II, 326-327. Italics mine.
19. Luther, "On Translating: An Open Letter," *Works of Martin Luther,* V, 10.
20. *Ibid.,* V, 15. See also Joachim Jeremias, *The Central Message of the New Testament* (New York: Charles Scribner's Sons, 1965), p. 55.
21. *Works of Martin Luther,* V, 20.
22. Whale, *The Protestant Tradition,* p. 44.
23. *Ibid.*
24. Reinhold Niebuhr, *Man's Nature and His Communities:* Essays on the dynamics and enigmas of man's personal and social existence (New York: Charles Scribner's Sons, 1965), p. 119.
25. Article IV: Of Justification, *Augsburg Confession,* in *Triglot Concordia:* The Symbolical Books of the Ev. Lutheran Church (St. Louis: Concordia Publishing House, 1921), p. 45.

26. Jaroslav Pelikan, *From Luther to Kierkegaard:* A Study in the History of Theology (St. Louis: Concordia Publishing House, 1950), p. 33. See also p. 60.
27. *Ibid.,* p. 42.
28. Williston Walker, *A History of the Christian Church,* Revised Edition (New York: Charles Scribner's Sons, 1959), p. 334.
29. *The Formula of Concord,* Thorough Declaration, in *Triglot Concordia,* p. 917. Cf. *Apology of the Augsburg Confession, ibid.,* p. 121.
30. Pelikan, *op. cit.,* p. 44.
31. *Ibid.,* p. 69.
32. Sven Göransson, "Ortodoxien," *Nordisk Teologisk Uppslagsbok* (Lund: C. W. K. Gleerups Förlag; Copenhagen: Ejnar Munksgaard, 1952), II, 1403-1404.
33. N. H. Söe, "Pietism," *op. cit.,* III, 57-58.
34. Hjalmar Lindroth, "Rättfärdiggörelse," *op. cit.,* III, 437.
35. *Ibid.*
36. Cf. Pelikan, *From Luther to Kierkegaard,* pp. 45-58.
37. Lindroth, *op. cit.,* III, 438.
38. Ragnar Bring, "Justification," *The Encyclopedia of the Lutheran Church,* ed. Julius Bodensieck (Minneapolis: Augsburg Publishing House, 1965), II, 1193.
39. Bring, "Justification," *Encyclopedia of the Lutheran Church,* II, 1194.
40. *Ibid.,* II, 1192.
41. *Ibid.,* II, 1194.
42. Hans Küng, *Justification: The Doctrine of Karl Barth and a Catholic Reflection,* translated by Thomas Collins, Edmund E. Tolk, and David Granskou (New York: Thomas Nelson & Sons, 1964).
43. Karl Barth's letter in Küng, *op. cit.,* p. xx.
44. *Justification Today:* Studies and Reports. Published and Edited by the Commission and Department of Theology as Supplement to No. 1, 1965, *Lutheran World,* Publication of the Lutheran World Federation. (Copies available at $.75 per copy from National Lutheran Council, 50 Madison Avenue, New York 10010.)
45. *Time,* August 23, 1963, p. 48.
46. *Justification Today,* cf. p. 15.
47. *Ibid.,* p. 30.
48. *Ibid.,* see pp. 18, 25.
49. *Ibid.,* p. 32.

50. *Ibid.,* see p. 50.

51. *Ibid.,* p. 58.

52. Howard Clark Kee, Franklin W. Young, Karlfried Froehlich, *Understanding the New Testament,* Second edition (Englewood Cliffs, N.J.: Prentice-Hall, Inc., 1965), p. 197.

53. D. E. H. Whiteley, *The Theology of St. Paul* (Philadelphia: Fortress Press, 1964), p. 160.

54. *Ibid.*

55. Rudolf Bultmann, *Theology of the New Testament,* tr. Kendrick Grobel (New York: Charles Scribner's Sons, 1951), 1, 272.

56. *Ibid.,* I, 276.

57. *Ibid.,* I, 272, 277.

58. *Ibid.,* I, 314.

59. *Ibid.,* I, 314-317.

60. Joachim Jeremias, *The Central Message of the New Testament,* p. 54.

61. *Ibid.,* p. 57.

62. *Ibid.,* p. 64.

63. *Ibid.*

64. Luther, "A Treatise on the Holy Sacrament of Baptism," *Works of Martin Luther,* I, 57, 59-60.

65. Jeremias, *op. cit.,* p. 65.

66. *Ibid.,* p. 59.

CHAPTER IV

1. Luther, *W.A.* 56. 204.14. Cited by Gordon Rupp, *The Righteousness of God,* p. 171.

2. Ragnar Bring, "Justification," *Encyclopedia of the Lutheran Church,* II, 1190.

3. Jeremias, *The Central Message of the New Testament,* p. 64.

4. Bring *op. cit.,* II, 1188.

5. *Ibid.,* II, 1194.

6. Luther, *W.A.* 56. 226.24. Cited by Rupp. *The Righteousness of God,* pp. 169-170.

7. Luther, *W.A.* 56. 225.15; 226.18; 251.12. Cited by Rupp, *op. cit.,* p. 169.

8. See John A. Bollier, "The Righteousness of God," *Interpretation,* Vol. VIII, No. 4 (October, 1954), p. 411. Bollier's article insists on the theocentric understanding of the righteousness of God in Paul.